# Resound

## SEVEN CONFESSIONS
## FROM PORTLAND

Published in Beaverton, Oregon, by Good Catch Publishing.
www.goodcatchpublishing.com
V1.1

*Printed in the United States of America*

# TABLE OF CONTENTS

# Acknowledgements

I would like to thank Luke Reid for his vision for this book and Marissa Price for her hard work in making it a reality. And to the people of Resound, thank you for your boldness and vulnerability in sharing your personal stories.

This book would not have been published without the amazing efforts of our project manager and editor, Hayley Pandolph. Her untiring resolve pushed this project forward and turned it into a stunning victory. Thank you for your great fortitude and diligence. Deep thanks to our incredible Editor in Chief, Michelle Cuthrell, and Executive Editor, Jen Genovesi, for all the amazing work they do. I would also like to thank our invaluable proofreader, Melody Davis, for the focus and energy she has put into perfecting our words.

Lastly, I want to extend our gratitude to the creative and very talented Jenny Randle, who designed the beautiful cover for *Resound: Seven Confessions from Portland.*

Daren Lindley
President and CEO
Good Catch Publishing

The book you are about to read
is a compilation of authentic life stories.
The facts are true, and the events are real.
These storytellers have dealt with crisis, tragedy, abuse
and neglect and have shared their most private moments,
mess-ups and hang-ups in order for others to learn and
grow from them. In order to protect the identities of those
involved in their pasts, the names and details of some
storytellers have been withheld or changed.

# Introduction

What do you do when life is careening out of control? When addiction has overtaken you or abuse chained you with fear? Is depression escapable? Will relationships ever be healthy again? Are we destined to dissolve into an abyss of sorrow? Or will the sunlight of happiness ever return?

Your life can change. It is possible to become a new person. The seven stories you are about to read prove that people right here in our town have stopped dying and started living. Whether they've been beaten by abuse, broken promises, shattered dreams or suffocating addictions, the resounding answer is, "Yes! You can become a new person." The potential to break free from gloom and into a bright future awaits you.

Expect inspiration, hope and transformation! As you walk through the pages of this book with fellow Portlanders, you will not only find riveting accounts of their hardships; you will learn the secrets that brought about their breakthrough. These people are no longer living in the shadows of yesterday; they are thriving with a sense of mission and purpose TODAY.

May these stories inspire you to do the same.

# Through the Eyes of a Child
## The Story of Greg Roid
### Written by Douglas Abbott

I stood in the bathroom looking at a dead man. He looked back at me from the mirror over the sink. The eyes were muddy with dread, waiting for the death that had been assigned but hadn't yet arrived, like a joke with a delayed punch line. A corpse waiting to happen. As I looked at my reflection, my gaze lingered on the morbid swells under my jaw where my lymph nodes — the routing stations of my undoing — bulged with their corrupted contents. There were other ghastly growths under my arms, in my abdomen and in my groin. The cancer was all over my body. The chances of beating it back with chemotherapy were too minuscule to be taken seriously.

"Honey, are you okay?" Keri called from the living room.

"Fine, sweetheart!" I lied, my voice echoing off the porcelain fixtures. "I'll be right out."

I ran some water to make my bathroom visit sound legitimate. I couldn't bring myself to share my abysmal outlook with my wife. She was already frightened enough. I think I was doing the chemo just to give her some hope and relief.

"Okay, but hurry! Dinner's ready."

# Resound

I hesitated at the mirror, reflecting on the fact that my diagnosis had come on my 27th birthday, of all days. Happy birthday. The timing rang with a note of finality — birth and death, synchronized neatly on the calendar. The fact that I wasn't actually dead yet didn't seem to matter. The time I had left, rather than being an opportunity to enjoy a few more experiences, was nothing but the run-up to the final frame — a period during which my fate would announce itself implacably with every look in the mirror, every uncomfortable bulge, every sympathetic word from a friend. Even if I could withstand all that, any residue of vitality I might otherwise enjoy would be wrested away from me by the chemotherapy. The foul chemicals would turn me into a walking waste. If the disease didn't get me, the treatment would.

I wondered what dying was going to feel like …

❧❧❧

I grew up in Roseburg, Oregon, a town of 21,000 souls, which at the time was the timber capital of the United States. It was presumed that if you grew up there, you would take your generational place at the mill or, if you were the stalwart type, work as a lumberjack.

"Daddy is moving out," my mom announced to my sister and me when I was 6. At the time, we were gathered in the living room for a family conference. It was a standard drizzly Oregon morning in April 1969.

"Your father and I fell out of love," Mom explained.

# Through the Eyes of a Child

This was only vaguely meaningful to my 6-year-old mind. She was so matter-of-fact about the whole thing that I didn't process what was happening at first. Furthermore, I got to see my dad regularly afterward, so it wasn't until Mom remarried and my stepfather, Mike, moved in that it started to sink in that someone had blown up my family. The house took on a surreal aftermarket feel for a time, during which my schoolwork slipped.

"Gregory! Why aren't you doing your schoolwork?" Mom confronted me. I had always been an obedient child.

"Are you sad about Dad being gone?" she asked, ruffling my hair. I nodded miserably.

"Don't worry, Gregory. He's still going to come and see you. And Mike loves you. He's going to be a good father to you and Valerie."

My father continued to be a part of my life. Meanwhile, Mike was a good stepfather to us. Some parents establish boundaries to keep their children from inconveniencing them; Mike established them to prepare us for life. He treated us like his biological children. He often brought us along on outdoor excursions and taught us how to hunt and fish, which I enjoy to this day.

❧❧❧

I was shy all through school and remained unattached romantically, even in high school. However, that didn't stop me from participating in Roseburg's time-honored leisure activity of choice: kegger parties. These were epic events that could involve 15 to 20 kegs of beer, live bands and colossal bonfires, with the entire high school in attendance. Because it was tradition, the parties drew little more than an occasional angry speech from objecting authority figures.

I found a favorable niche in school sports due to a natural athletic ability and a large frame. (By the time I was full grown, I was 6 feet tall and weighed 225 pounds.) Football was a no-brainer, particularly since I expected it to help me procure a scholarship or two, which was my only chance of going to college. During high school, I dug into my studies and finished with a 3.85 GPA.

While I was still in my senior year, my left knee was destroyed by a hard tackle during football practice. Afterward, the knee was a mess of disconnected tissue that would require surgery and a long, painful rehabilitation. The injury derailed my plans to attend college and left me with little interest in life for a time. My schoolwork began slipping badly.

During this time, my science instructor, Mr. McBee, saw what was happening and helped prod me through a grueling science project. He stopped me as I was leaving class one day.

"I know what you're going through," he told me. He was trying to be casual, but it didn't quite come off. He was sitting on the very corner of his desk in a position that must have been uncomfortable to the point of being painful. I might have laughed, but I was too depressed. Besides, I could hear the compassion in his voice.

# Through the Eyes of a Child

"So football isn't going to happen for you now. So what? There's something better waiting for you. Let me tell you something. When I was a young man, I had my career all planned out, down to the day. I was going to be an award-winning biologist and study grizzly bears. Then I got bit by one, and it was back to the drawing board. I was lucky the thing wasn't in the mood for a buffet lunch!

"This injury may have taken your knee, but don't let it take your spirit, boy!" he told me. "There's a lot more inside you than athletic ability. It's up to you to find it."

I have no idea if Mr. McBee knew how much his words helped me rebound after my injury. When I finally submitted my term project, Mr. McBee complimented me on it, though he marked it down because of tardiness. "Would have been an 'A' if you'd handed it in on time," he told me.

꩜꩜꩜

After graduation I started working, first as a meat cutter and later at the local mill, where I spent my days moving huge sheets of lumber through the milling stages. It was around this time, about age 20, that I met Keri.

Shy as I was, I can't imagine how the two of us clicked, particularly since I knew beforehand that we were the focus of a matchmaking effort by a close friend of mine, Lynn, who had recommended her to me. One evening we were both invited to a small party at Lynn's house.

I saw her mingling with a handful of guests in Lynn's

living room when I arrived. She looked alluring in faded blue jeans and a pink middy sweater. She was working on a small plate of Bagel Bites and a beer. She managed to make eating look attractive. There was something simple and honest about her. She was tapping her foot to the classic rock music that was throbbing from the speakers.

"I remember you from Mr. Klein's civics class," Keri told me after I had inserted myself into the circle and introductions had been made.

"Yeah, I remember you, too. I always wanted to ask you out for dinner."

She smiled. "Well, why didn't you?"

Ironically, I found it easy to take to Keri knowing that our meeting had been arranged. I found, happily, that Keri was adorable and great fun to be around, so I looked for any excuse I could find to be with her. Within a year we were living together, first in Eugene and then in Albany, where I worked as an apprentice meat cutter while Keri worked for a hand therapist.

We were married in 1986. Whether it was in deference to tradition or some latent spirituality, Keri wanted to be married in a church. As it happened, there was a church there in Albany she had come to admire — a small white A-frame nestled in fir trees. Its sanctuary greeted the street with lovely stained-glass windows. The pastor didn't know us very well but was quite amenable about marrying us, so we said our wedding vows there after going through a stint of premarital counseling.

While we were still living in Albany, Keri and I ran

into an old friend of hers named Shelly at the grocery store.

"Where are you living these days?" Keri asked after introductions.

"We're living up in Monmouth," Shelly answered, indicating her husband, Troy, who was nearby inspecting nectarines and loading them into a bag. "We've been attending a great church up there. Why don't you come up for a service sometime?"

So we made the drive up one Sunday and hung out with Shelly, Troy and some of their friends over coffee and doughnuts after the service. Keri and I both felt a pleasant kinship with them and started making regular trips to Monmouth for services and Bible studies. Soon we were settled into a small group, whose facilitator, Todd, was attending seminary.

Because we got on well with Todd and the others, Keri and I followed most of them to the church he began to pastor — Mountain View Baptist Church. We both saw church involvement as a pleasant enough way to spend part of the week, but we had no explicit convictions about God.

My only meaningful exposure to Christianity thus far had come through my biological father, who became a Christian when I was around 21. At the time, I knew something profound had happened to him, because he changed visibly. He was always giving me cassette tapes or books on the subject. I was affected enough to have a conversation about it with a close friend, Jim.

"I'm not sure what to make of this Christianity thing," I told Jim. "Is it really much different from all these other religions?"

Jim shrugged. "I don't know. Jesus sure got a raw deal. All he did was go around helping people, and he got strung up for it."

"I'm not sure about religion, period. A lot of people get pretty weird on it. Remember the Rainbow People?"

"Well, there's the answer to your first question." Jim turned his palm up. "I'd say they're a lot different from Christians. Most of the Christians I meet seem like pretty decent people."

I had nothing against religious devotion but didn't care to undergo the kind of mesmerizing transformation I had seen in some of these people, who always seemed to have lost something vital in the process. At the same time, there was something enormously intriguing about my father's zeal for God. The peace and fulfillment I'd seen in him planted a seed in me that lay dormant for several years.

Now, my direct involvement with Mountain View Baptist Church was forcing a reckoning with the words of God. After Keri and I had been attending for a few months, I started leading a small group Bible study. My pastor gave me weekly topics, and I fleshed them out through my own examination of scripture.

I had never spent a great deal of time reading the Bible. Now the story of Jesus was squarely before me. I discovered that my ideas about the gospel were mostly based on secondhand impressions that focused mainly on the moral teachings of Jesus, a collection of strict imperatives I had often found intimidating. Now, however, I saw in the Biblical account a man who lived a selfless life like no other, continually pouring his energy into helping others. He went around healing, blessing and guiding everyone he encountered. More than once, he turned down opportunities to use his fame and popularity to seize political power. I could find no instance where he had enjoyed any personal gain from his ministry, material or otherwise. To a man who told Jesus he would follow him, Jesus warned: "Foxes have holes and birds of the air have nests, but [the man you see before you] has no place to lay his head" (Matthew 8:20). In carrying out his life's work, he endured insults, misunderstanding, rejection, betrayal. In the end, he died an unimaginably horrible death. The crux of the matter was that if he was God, he had submitted to all this willingly, since he had the power to avoid any of it he pleased. But he hadn't. He had gone through with it — for *me*. There was nothing in it for him except public humiliation and cataclysmic pain.

I had seen enough in my life to convince me of humanity's need for redemption. The gravity of the world's gnarled affairs made Christ's offer particularly compelling to me.

The more I read, the more I was convinced the Biblical account was true. There was no great burst of illumination; ironically, as I consumed the scriptures, my intellect relaxed. In its place, a quiet confidence grew inside me. I began to see the story of Christ through the eyes of a child.

I felt strongly that I needed to formalize my belief in Christ. A prayer had to be prayed; words had to be spoken. I seized the moment on a quiet afternoon while I was alone in my study.

"Jesus," I prayed aloud, "thank you for showing me who you are and the sacrifice you made for me. I need you in my life. I need your forgiveness and healing. I am entrusting my life to your care. Help me change for the better and live for you. Teach me what it means to follow you. I am yours!"

It wasn't long before I realized I needed to be baptized, following the example of Jesus, who was himself baptized. I wanted to seal my decision by making a public profession of my belief in Christ.

Keri desired the same things I did, so we were both baptized on an obligingly clear spring morning in May of 1988. The church was full in spite of the unseasonably warm weather.

"What does Christ mean to you?" Pastor Todd asked as I stood in waist-deep water. The pastor was on my left and a strapping deacon named Jack was on my right; since I weighed 235 pounds, they had brought out the big guns to immerse me.

"He is the Savior of the world," I answered. "Now he's mine. I'm giving my life to him." I heard people cheering at my words and saw Keri sporting a huge grin as she waited at the side for her turn. They dunked me, and I came up out of the water feeling like a 12-year-old boy on Christmas morning. The sun streaming in through the stained-glass windows bounced off the water in colorful shards. I felt the eternal significance of the moment as I watched Keri in turn go under the water.

It was a time of discovery. Keri and I dug into our marriage and enjoyed the close-knit fellowship of our Bible study group, which met together several times each week for meals, board games and even trips to the coast. I had never had such a group of friends before. Keri and I were having the time of our lives.

I had no inkling of the ordeal that lay ahead.

❧❧❧

In the fall of 1989, Keri and I sat down to dinner on a rain-cooled Friday evening. We had the whole weekend to visit and catch up.

"How are things at the office?" I asked through a mouthful of garlic bread.

"Fine," she said. "Busy. Lots of surgeries. We were booked solid between July and October."

"Great! I'm not surprised. You do good work. *I'd* come to you for hand therapy."

Keri smiled. "How did things go at the doctor's?"

I had scheduled a visit to investigate a lump in my groin. "Fine. He took a look and said I had nothing to worry about. Said it was just an enlarged gland and it would go away."

"Good." Keri smiled again and took a sip of Chianti.

But it didn't go away. Eight months later, it had actually grown, so I scheduled an appointment with a urologist who looked at me, poked around a bit and then told me he was referring me to an internist.

"You won't get in to see an internist for six months," Keri told me. "This isn't good."

However, in a strange confluence of events, I saw both the internist and the oncologist on the same day. Usually appointments weren't scheduled for months. I knew it was divine intervention when my doctor, who only came around to a specific office once a month, was available to see me.

The oncologist introduced himself as Doctor O. "Much easier than pronouncing my name, which has 17 syllables in it," he joked. Then he proceeded to poke me some more.

"This could be Hodgkin's disease, or it could be lymphoma," he told me.

"People die from Hodgkin's disease," I said with some alarm.

The oncologist gave me a somber look. "People die from lymphoma, too," he informed me.

"What's lymphoma?"

"Cancer of the lymph nodes."

*Cancer.* It didn't seem real. I was only 27 years old.

They scheduled a biopsy. Meanwhile, I went around in a strange fog for several days, ruminating that serious illness wasn't supposed to strike until people were at least

50. Then, one day, I arrived home after a long day at work. Keri was sitting in the dining room. She wasn't eating or drinking or reading, or even petting the cat. She was just sitting there waiting for me. Something in her eyes made the flesh on my neck crawl. Finally she spoke: "Did Doctor O call you?"

"No."

"He didn't call you?"

"No. What is it?"

But I already knew. The biopsy had come back. It was cancer. Worse, it was Stage IV cancer, spread all through my body. The most bizarre thing of all was that, after piecing the sequence of events back together, I discovered that Doctor O had called me about the cancer. However, I had no recollection of the conversation.

I tried to process what was happening, but it didn't really hit home until my chemotherapy treatments were scheduled. Then it was official. I had watched people go through chemotherapy. Just the mention of the word evoked stark images of gaunt, hairless people with gray flesh, plodding around in hospital robes, eating yogurt and plain oatmeal to keep from vomiting.

"Sweetheart, it's going to be all right," Keri told me. But I could see the terror in her eyes. I knew the rule that when things are bad, the people who love you have to say comforting things to you, even when they don't entirely believe them.

I expected to die from my illness — or perhaps be sick for the remainder of my life. In my mind, I ticked off the reasons why I was finished: 1) my cancer was in the most advanced stage, having spread from my neck all the way down to my knees; 2) it was inoperable; 3) chemotherapy was a last-ditch effort to save someone who has nearly succumbed to cancer already, and its success rate was low; 4) I could die from the chemotherapy even if the cancer was eliminated.

My doctor had explained to me that cancer is a condition in which the body begins producing morbid tissue. If it isn't caught in time, as in my case, the whole body is overrun by diseased tissues. Eventually, some vital organ fails, and death occurs. My wife researched it and learned that 1,500 people die of cancer every *day.*

Keri and I attended a Sunday service at our church a day before my first chemotherapy treatment. We got to the service and settled into our seats. After worship, Pastor Todd moved to the lectern to make the announcements. After the usual dry list of schedule changes, bake sales and such, he addressed the group about my illness.

"Church, I'm asking all of you to keep Greg and Keri Roid in your prayers. Greg has been diagnosed with Stage IV lymphoma and has just begun chemotherapy."

I heard several people making sympathetic sounds. Then a lady named Nora spoke from the back of the church.

"Shouldn't we lay hands on Greg and pray for him now?" she said. "It says in James 5, 'Is any one of you sick? He should call the elders of the church to pray over him and anoint him with oil in the name of the Lord. And the prayer offered in faith will make the sick person well. The Lord will raise him up.'"

This was a Baptist church. Most of the members were undemonstrative in their worship. However, Nora was not typical in any sense. She was at least 90 years old. She wore glasses that rested on the tip of her nose and was constantly peering at you over them, like a stern schoolteacher. She always wore her white hair back in a bun with a knitting needle through it. Her dresses were no-nonsense numbers made of some miracle fabric that still looked the same after 500 washings. She had never been married.

Whenever I think of Nora, I think of Anna, the old prophetess in the Bible, who lived at the Temple and spent her days fasting and praying (Luke 2). Nora may not have lived at the church, but she was definitely a prayer warrior, and she was there whenever the doors were open, whether it was a service, a car wash or a bit of spring cleaning. She was like part of the building.

"Nora is right," Pastor Todd agreed. "We need to pray for Greg. Worship team, come down and join us. I want everyone to gather around Greg right now."

And they did. A minute later, I was surrounded by people. Hands were on my shoulders, back, arms and chest. I could hear them whispering. Some of them sang softly. Pastor Todd stood directly in front of me, put his hand on the top of my head and began praying in a strong voice.

"Lord, we lift Greg up to you to be healed, in full

confidence that you are willing and able to accomplish it. The book of James tells us we are right to do this! As the passage says, 'Is anyone among you sick? Let him call the elders of the church to pray over him and anoint him with oil in the name of the Lord. And the prayer offered in faith will make the sick person well' (James 5:14-15). We find encouragement in Isaiah 53: 'By his stripes we are healed.' And again in Exodus 15: 'I am the Lord, who heals you.' When you walked the earth as a man, you went around healing everyone who came to you. We trust that Christ is the purest expression of your good will toward us and ask for you to make our brother Greg whole and healthy again."

There was more, and for the first few minutes, I felt very uncomfortable. I had never seen a prayer huddle, and now I was in the *middle* of one. Then I began to feel touched as the prayer continued. There was love coming through their hands.

As I listened intently to the pastor's words, I realized that my perception about healing didn't match up with what was written in the Bible. Since I had trusted Christ as Savior and even before, I had kept the notion of healing in its own mystical category in my mind, far removed from real life in the modern world. I heard stories of healing and lumped them in with all other supernatural events — untraceable, not provable and without explanation. I believed healings either no longer occurred, or they were simply unavailable to most people. This seemed reasonable considering that I had never witnessed a healing nor spoken to anyone who had, Christian or otherwise. I figured God didn't heal people anymore, or if he did, it was rare and had nothing to do with our prayers or our understanding of scripture.

"… we believe your hand is outstretched, longing to heal, Father. We celebrate your good character, which is to always have mercy. You are a God of renewal …"

While I stood there, with 30 people gripping me and singing over me, I felt a great peace welling up inside me. Something was drawing me to relax my mind and trust God. As I did, I saw an image of a little boy clasping the hand of his father as they walked along the beach. The boy was smiling up at his father, his eyes full of admiration and trust. In his face and in his posture, there was no indication the boy was afraid or in pain. This was a child who had no inkling of hunger or want of any kind. In him was a fierce confidence that his dad was going to make everything come out right.

I remembered the time of study and prayer that had culminated in my baptism. It had been a time of discovery when years of hurts and betrayals and cynicism had fallen off me as I approached God with the simple trust of a child. I remembered some of Christ's words that had jumped off the page at me: "Let the little children come to me, and do not hinder them. For I tell you that the kingdom of heaven belongs to such as these" (Matthew 19:14).

Somehow I knew God was inviting me to trust him in this moment. I began to say to myself: *Jesus is going to heal me. I know it. He's really going to do it. I'm going to be healed. My Savior is going to take this cancer out of me. I'm going to live. I'm going to be well again.*

Suddenly, I felt a warm tingling begin inside my chest and spread out into my limbs and through my extremities, like the flaring of a match head. I was at peace, and my body seemed to have no weight for a time, as though I were suspended in seawater, warmed by the sun. I could still hear my church fellows praying and humming over me.

Then Pastor Todd finished his prayer, and we all returned to our seats for the rest of the service.

"Something really strange happened to me back there," I told Keri in the car on the drive home.

"When we were praying for you?"

I nodded. "I felt this warm sensation in my chest and then all through my body. I felt like I was floating. It was incredible."

Keri didn't say much, but I could tell she was chewing on it. I was, too.

సౌసౌసౌ

My first chemotherapy session left me feeling dull, weak and slightly ill.

"One down, nine to go," I told Keri.

We drove to a friend's house for a game of basketball two days later. The pastor's wife, Martha, came up to me after the game. She was looking at me intently.

# Through the Eyes of a Child

"Come here, Greg." She lifted her hand to my neck.

"The lumps on your neck are gone," she declared. She pressed the hollow under my chin gently, first on one side, then the other. "They're gone!" she said again.

My lymph nodes had been swollen for weeks.

She put her hands on my shoulders and looked up at me. "How are you feeling?"

"Fine." I shrugged.

Martha was in the medical field, so she had my attention at this point. I excused myself and went into the bathroom. I checked my groin and felt under my arms. No lumps. I turned and looked at myself in the mirror, as if I could get a second opinion from the person there, who was looking back at me with amazement.

The following Monday, I went back for my second round of chemo.

"How are we doing?" Doctor O asked cursorily.

"Doing great!" I said heartily.

He gave me a curious look and nodded sidewise at me. "Good," he said. But I caught a bit of puzzlement in his eyes. Here was a Stage IV lymphoma patient just starting to enjoy his chemotherapy, giving him a wide grin and saying he was on top of the world. It must have seemed out of place.

"Let's have a look at you," he said, setting my chart down.

His brow creased almost imperceptibly as he started probing around my neck. I kept quiet for a minute as he continued on to my armpits.

"Can you feel any lumps?" I asked him finally. I couldn't hold my tongue any longer.

"No," he said. His forehead creased a bit more as he continued his work. Finally, he folded his arms and just looked at me for a moment.

"Well?" I prompted. "Are there lumps anywhere?"

"No," he said, after a pause. He seemed to be stuck.

"This kind of thing doesn't happen, does it?"

"No," he said again, as though his vocabulary had been reduced to one word.

Finally, he took a deep breath and forged on. "Well, Mr. Roid, quite honestly, I don't understand what happened."

"I'll *tell* you what happened," I said. "My church prayed over me. Healed me."

"What?!"

"Yes. My whole church gathered around me and laid hands on me. They prayed over me for — I don't know, 15 minutes. Then two days later, I noticed the lumps were gone."

I could see his mind racing behind his eyes. "Do you think that really happened?"

"Yeah, I do. Do you have any other explanation? Chemotherapy doesn't get rid of Stage IV cancer with one treatment, does it?"

"No, it doesn't," he admitted.

In the days and weeks following, I began to question what had actually happened. Was the prayer of my church instrumental? Did the chemotherapy session simply have extravagant results? Was it a combination of both? Were the lumps cancerous to begin with? My intellect struggled with my spirit.

In the end, I couldn't dismiss the evidence at hand. More importantly, I couldn't forget what had happened when my church prayed for me — the warmth in my chest, the feeling of weightlessness, the rapture of the moment. Somehow, I knew. God had come through for me.

∼∼∼

After the cancer ordeal, Keri and I opened our home to several foster children. One of them, José, became our son by adoption. Before he came our way, he was abused, neglected and abandoned by his birth parents. Then he ricocheted through 13 foster homes before finally ending up in our care. José struggled with terrible anger and social isolation, but we loved him through all of it. He straightened out beautifully and became a state trooper with the California Highway Patrol.

Keri and I divorced in 2001. Our parting was amicable and without regret.

The years have been good to me, bringing more adventure than sorrow. I realized this with gratitude as I sat down to dinner recently with an old friend. Tony is from my hometown, Roseburg, and still lives there. He was surprised when I told him Keri and I had divorced.

"We grew apart," I said. "It happens. But I remarried a

few years ago. Stephanie is the reason I went back to church. I know you don't believe in marriages made in heaven, but Stephanie makes a strong case."

"How so?"

"I was attending a Kenny Chesney concert in Portland when I ran into her. You don't know her, but she's from Roseburg, too, although she moved away not long after I did. We both moved around quite a bit over the years, but we were both living in Portland when I ran into her at the concert.

"Before I had even found my seat, I went to the concession window to get some snacks. While I was standing in line, I saw Stephanie go by. It's a pretty big auditorium, and it's kind of weird that I recognized her after more than 20 years, not to mention glimpsing her in a sea of people like that. Maybe not worth writing *Unsolved Mysteries* about just yet, but stay with me.

"I yelled her name, she turned around and came back, and we stood in the concession line reminiscing. She remembered me from Roseburg High, too. Then, after we got our snacks, we went to find our seats together. We pulled our tickets out, and d*** if her seat wasn't *right next* to mine. Now, get this — the Rose Garden has 20,000 seats! I looked it up. And the concert was pretty near sold out."

"How about that," Tony said dryly. He looked like he wanted to be somewhere else. Tony is a self-proclaimed agnostic and not exactly a romantic fellow. In fact, he's a certified lonely guy.

"Wait! There's more. Stephanie told me later that when I spotted her in the corridor, she was coming from the restroom. She says it was the weirdest thing, but when she finished up in the restroom, she washed her hands *twice*."

"So?" Tony said, shaking his head.

"So, the corridor was behind me. I wasn't walking backward through the line. I just happened to be turning around and gawking behind me when Stephanie walked by. The timing was precise. If she hadn't washed her hands twice …"

Tony was kind of looking at me sideways. "That's some story, all right. So what made you want to tell *me* about it? Like you said, I don't believe in soul mates and all that. Stranger things have happened."

"I knew you were going to say that! Can you really sit there and tell me that you think all those things happened by chance?"

Tony shrugged. "Who am I to say? All I know is, I used to pray for a wife all the time. Didn't happen. So I stopped praying."

"Well, maybe you should pick it back up again."

Just then, the doorbell rang. It was my friends John and Rita Vater.

"Tony, meet John and Rita. They're small group leaders at Resound Church."

A round of handshakes followed.

"Tony is from my hometown," I said, for the benefit of John and Rita.

"Tony, why don't you come by for a service while you're in town?" John suggested.

"I don't really do church," Tony said politely.

"Well, maybe we can change your mind. First-time visitors are treated like family. Come twice and we'll treat you to a sumptuous feast."

I must have smirked, because John gave me a discreet wink.

I was still thinking about Tony that evening when Stephanie jarred me from my reverie by running her fingernails along the back of my neck.

"Penny for your thoughts."

I turned and regarded her with amazement. After several years of marriage and many more years of friendship before that, the woman can still sneak up on me whenever she feels like it.

"Tony came over this afternoon."

"Really? How's he doing?"

I shrugged. "He's still Tony. The way he talks, it's like suffering is his lot in life. But he'll come around. John and Rita came by while he was here today."

"Did John invite him to church?"

"Of course. You know John."

She nodded, and I saw a faraway look in her eyes. No doubt she was thinking about when we had first met John and Rita. That was an unprecedented time of growth and discovery for both of us.

We had recently moved back to Portland after years away. Both of us sensed God was telling us to find a good church, so we located a medium-sized congregation not far away from our house and began attending Sunday services there.

After we had been attending for a couple of months, we arrived about 25 minutes late one Sunday after grappling with vehicle issues the entire morning. We had just settled into our seats when the pastor walked to the front of the platform for the announcements.

My attention was wandering a bit, but then the pastor said something that caught my attention: "Ladies and gentlemen, when you attend services, please be respectful and be in your seats promptly at 10:15." The pastor's features were tight, and he was looking directly at Stephanie and me.

"I'm not going back to that place," I told Stephanie the second we were in the car after the service. Stephanie agreed and mentioned that a friend had recommended another church and had even given her a brochure. Her friend said the people there were friendly. Stephanie handed me the literature for Resound when we got home. I gave the brochure a cursory look. It looked good, but I couldn't be sure without checking it out in person.

"This doesn't really tell us anything, does it?" I said. "We really have to check it out."

Stephanie agreed, and we attended the following Sunday.

The church met in a movie theater. At first I thought it was funny. I whispered jokes to Stephanie about passing the popcorn while the service was getting underway. But before long, I discovered that I felt very relaxed. Most of the people around us seemed to be perfectly at ease. Around a dozen people came over and shook our hands when the music finished.

I was cynical enough to know that every church did this type of thing, but there was something in their eyes that conveyed a genuine interest. There was warmth and positive energy about them.

After the service, our escape was blocked by none other than John and Rita Vater, who positioned themselves strategically at the exit and waited for us.

"Hey, there!" John boomed like we were old friends. "I don't think I've seen you two in here before. My name's John. This is my wife, Rita."

The physical problem of the four of us all trying to shake each other's hands in the tight space was comical rather than awkward. We were enjoying ourselves, and there was no possibility of chalking up John and Rita's overture to something dutiful — they seemed to be having a better time than we were and proved it by standing there chatting us up for 20 minutes, asking about our work, and what part of Portland we called home.

"Why don't you come have some lunch on us?" John said as soon as the talk began to taper off.

"Thank you! But, no, we've got a pretty full day ahead of us." I squirmed a bit, reflecting silently that we had nothing of the kind. I couldn't tell them that I felt strange about letting two people buy us lunch whom we had known for all of 20 minutes.

# Through the Eyes of a Child

"All right, but at least take a rain check!" John reached to shake my hand again.

Stephanie and I didn't think twice about coming back on successive Sundays. We knew two things: 1) God had nudged us to find a church; and 2) we had found the friendliest, most laidback church either of us could remember attending.

John and Rita kept asking us to lunch, long past the point where normal people would have given up. Finally, we ran out of excuses and went.

The warm energy of the church was more than enough to keep us coming back, but I was about to get an upgrade.

After we had been attending for a month or so, John approached us about joining the Connections team. I had never occupied a service position in any church and felt no particular inclination to start now. I was less than enthusiastic about it.

"C'mon, you really don't know what you're missing," John said with a twinkle in his eye. "Connections is what I do. Let me ask you: Do I appear bored or tired to you?"

"No," I admitted. To the contrary, he almost always seemed energetic and fully engaged.

"I admit I wasn't too big on the idea myself." John made a sweeping gesture with his hand. "It just sounded like work, and I'm not the most sociable person that ever came down the pike."

I must have looked perplexed. John is one of the most charming people I've met at my church. It looks as though he's enjoying himself most of the time.

# Resound

"I like what I do," he said as if I'd spoken audibly. "You will, too. Trust me."

He was right. I do. I discovered that the energy I'd first noticed here was intensified as I went around helping others get into what our pastor calls the "whirlwind" of Resound. To use another comparison, the atmosphere here is like a bonfire on a beach. We already have a nice crackling fire going on. My job is to go around gathering driftwood to throw on it. The result is more warmth and light for everyone.

I'm glad to be a part of it.

# Alive Again
## The Story of David
### Written by Karen Koczwara

*How did I get here?*
*Am I dreaming?*

I rubbed my eyes groggily, confused by the protruding tubes and the beeping machines. As the room came into focus, I realized where I was.

*A hospital?*
*How did I get here?*
*What's going on?*

I wracked my fuzzy brain, desperately trying to recall the events that had led me to this bed. But my mind was as blank as the white hospital walls.

A few minutes later, the doctor strode in. "Do you know what happened?" he asked.

I shook my head, still confused.

*Was there an accident?*

"Your heart stopped. You were brought back to life and then underwent a quadruple bypass surgery."

*My heart stopped beating?*

Surely this must be a strange dream. Surely he must be talking to someone else. I was a healthy middle-aged guy. I exercised regularly and was in great shape. People thought I looked years younger than my age.

How could a guy like me have a heart attack and a massive surgery?

# Resound

I stared again at the tubes, stunned by the doctor's words. And slowly, the reality hit me with force.

*I died. And someone brought me back to life.*
*I should not be here right now.*
*I should be dead.*

❧❧❧

I was born on October 10, 1960 in Hicksville, New York, a small, newly developed bedroom community just outside Queens. My mother stayed home with my four siblings and me, while my father held a job as the airplane maintenance manager for American Airlines. The thriving airline provided ample opportunity for growth, and my father received many leadership awards during his career there.

As for me, life as a young boy in the early 60s was idyllic. I enjoyed playing baseball, riding bikes and chasing grasshoppers in the backyard. I stayed out with friends in the evening, laughing as we ran around until the sun disappeared. School was a pleasure, as I was filled with curiosity and loved creative activity. Overall, I was a happy kid from a pleasant home, grateful to be alive.

One night, when I was 8 years old, I lay awake on the bunk bed I shared with my brother, pondering the universe and the purpose of life. Suddenly, a thought struck me with such force that I could hardly breathe. I pictured the opposite of life — death — and imagined total blackness on the other side. Total aloneness, total separation from everyone and everything. The idea was frightening beyond words.

"Where do you go when you die?" I called out into the darkness to my brother. Three years my senior, he always knew how to make sense of things.

"You die and that's it," he replied matter-of-factly.

"But will you and me and Mom and Dad know each other after we're all dead someday?" I pressed, still troubled.

"No, you just die."

*You just die? So that's it? Nothing. Just total blackness. No love, no relationships.* I tried to picture it, but I couldn't. The notion was incomprehensible, horrid even. If there was simply darkness after death, what was the point of living? Suddenly struck by the futility of life, I began to weep softly in my bed. I'd never felt so disassociated and frightened before. Somehow, deep in my heart, I believed there must be something greater than myself, something holding the universe together. I was not satisfied with my brother's answer, and I was determined to find out the truth.

When I was 9 years old, my father announced our family was moving to Oklahoma for his work. I had seen enough Western movies to envision what it must look like — cowboys and Indians, sprawling green ranches and horses galloping along the winding roads. We packed our station wagon and made the long drive west. The trip took days, and we stopped several times to ask the country folk for directions. Soon, tumbleweeds and hot, dusty, barren land replaced the bustling cities of New York. A tinge of disappointment ran through me, as I realized our new surroundings were not quite what I'd pictured. *Now* this *is Hicksville,* I thought wryly.

We settled into our new home, and my father returned to work, putting in longer hours and making more money than ever before. A year after the move, he called us in one evening for a family meeting.

"Your mother and I are going to get divorced," he informed us. He delivered no explanation — just the dreaded, horrible words.

I burst into tears, torn apart at the news. My older brother became inconsolable as well. How could this happen? We'd just been one big happy family in the station wagon a few months earlier. Now we'd be torn apart, ripped in two and forced to pick sides. It just wasn't fair!

I moved with my siblings and mother to a farming community in the country, and we got an Irish Setter dog. My father lived an hour and a half away, where he continued to pour himself into his work. We saw little of him for the next several years. Every so often, I spotted him in the stands at my basketball games. I became distraught about his disappearance. Just like a ghost, he'd slipped out of our home and our lives and nearly vanished into thin air.

Though I stayed out of major trouble, I was a bit of a mouthy kid. It hadn't taken me long after moving to Oklahoma to figure out that we lived smack in the center of the Bible Belt. I poked fun at the conservative Christians and their music, convinced they'd been sucked into some sort of time warp and gone back in time a few decades. Since learning to play the guitar, music had become a vitally important part of my life. But the sort of stuff these churchy folks were into didn't appeal to me much. I had a style of my own.

I finished high school at age 16 and spent the next several years trying my hand at various entrepreneurial ventures. At 17, I moved to Colorado. The idea of trading the hot, dusty plains of Oklahoma for cool green terrain was appealing.

Two years later, a woman who had become like an aunt to me called me up. "I thought of you, David," she said. "My nephew just moved to Oklahoma, and he plays classical guitar. I know you play guitar as well. I thought maybe you two might hit it off."

As much as I enjoyed the Colorado scenery, I knew I wasn't doing anything significant with my life. I returned to Oklahoma and met up with the guy. We hit it off right away and began playing guitar together. We also wrote classical and jazz instrumental songs, and music became my foremost passion. It had been a form of therapy for me over the years, a way to release the emotions I could not often express otherwise. For a moment, when the guitar and I became one, the rest of the world slipped away, and nothing else mattered.

When I was 24, I attempted to reconnect with my father. I called him up, unsure of what to expect after so many years. I asked him if it would be okay for me to visit him. "I know it's been a long time," I told him. "I have a list of questions for you."

"Go ahead and ask away," my father replied.

One weekend, I went to see him. I asked my questions one by one. "Why did you leave? Did you know what impact that had on us? What was your father like? Who am I to you?" To my surprise, my father answered them honestly. We laughed and cried, and a sense of relief washed over me. My father led his own life these days, and I wasn't sure that included me. But at least I had some sense of closure for now.

I continued to play music and write songs. Inspired by my love for the art, I returned to school and completed University College at Oklahoma University with a degree in music composition. At last, I had a true sense of direction and purpose. There, I met a woman, and we began dating. She was from Belgium, and her father had moved to Oklahoma to start a business. I was impressed by her close relationship with her family, as I also held the same values. Things quickly grew serious.

On February 20, 1988, we married in a Catholic church. The priest who performed our ceremony told us shortly before the wedding, "You two are going to have lots of problems." I was startled by his bluntness. They weren't exactly the poetic words we'd been hoping for to jumpstart our new life together. But deep down, I wondered if he might be right.

My wife gave birth to a beautiful little boy we named

# Alive Again

Alex. I began a career as a creative director, producing corporate shows that included music. The job was a dream for me, as I finally had the opportunity to use the talents I'd been nurturing for so long. Around this time, we took a family trip to Vancouver, and I fell in love with the Northwest. There was something staggeringly beautiful about the tall pine trees, the crisp air and the rugged mountains of Washington and Oregon. Suddenly, it hit me with force. *I've never loved Oklahoma. I'm ready to leave that place once and for all.*

"If you like it up here, you might want to check out Beaverton," a local suggested. "It's a suburb of Portland, and you can get a really nice house there."

My wife agreed to the move, and we bought a place in Beaverton but continued to live in Oklahoma until we sorted out the logistics. I remained with my job but began working on starting my own business in Oregon. Having made several major moves over my lifetime, I was happy to finally have a place to call home. As a creative musician, I appreciated the inspiring beauty of my new surroundings. My wife gave birth to a little girl, Isabelle, in 1995, and for a while, life took on a steady, pleasant pace. But change brewed just around the corner, and things would not stay the same for long.

Alex began elementary school, and he struggled with his work. One day, the teacher called my wife and me in for a conference. "Your son is having a difficult time with his academics," she informed us, showing us a few samples of his work.

We listened carefully and then discussed our son's troubles when we got home. "I'm not sure what to do. He's really having a tough time in class," I lamented to my wife.

Our neighbor invited us over one day. He was a pastor at a local church, and his children attended the Christian school associated with another church in the area. "It might be a good fit for your son," he suggested. "But I should let you know that they prioritize slots for church members."

We thanked him and mulled over the idea. I wasn't too keen on the idea of going to church, but if it meant getting my son into a school that could drastically help him academically, perhaps it was worth the effort.

"Let's just go on Sunday and give it a shot," I told my wife. "It's not like we have to go forever."

She reluctantly agreed, and the following Sunday, we showed up in our best attire. I was raised Catholic as a young man, attending church occasionally, but had no recent church experience and no expectation when I walked through the doors. We took our place in the pews, and the pastor strode to the front of the room and opened his Bible. He began to read from the book, sharing how God loved each of us, had a plan for our lives and a place for us to call home for eternity. That place was heaven.

As I sat there, a very strange and wonderful thing took place. Suddenly, it was as if the entire stage was shrouded in a white light with the pastor standing beneath it. As I watched him read out of the Bible, I leaned forward, mesmerized by what I saw and heard. *Wow! This is it! This guy is reading out of a book that was written by the creator of the world!* The missing pieces came together as I realized that the very thing I'd searched for at 8 years old was now right before me. I'd been so troubled as I lay in my bunk bed, wondering if there was anything but darkness on the other side of death. Now, it all made perfect sense. Life did have purpose after all. And that purpose included having a relationship with God.

When the pastor prayed at the end of the service, asking if anyone would like to invite God into his or her heart, I prayed along with him. *God, please come into my life. I need you. I need a Savior. I know I've done wrong things, and I ask you to forgive me and cleanse me. Help me to live for you. Thank you.*

I felt wonderfully free and light as air as I headed home that day. I hadn't been searching for God at all when I'd stepped through those doors. Life had been treating me well, and I had no reason to believe I needed help. But God clearly met me in that moment, filling in the gaps and providing the answers I'd struggled to find as a child. He had known long before I had that this moment would come. I had showed up to church hoping to get my kid into a private school and walked out the doors a changed man. My life would never be the same.

I shared my thoughts with my wife, but she was not happy to hear it. "This is going to be a problem," she muttered, shaking her head.

My heart sank. We were clearly not on the same page.

I could only pray that God would open her eyes as he had mine. I would not let her disapproval squelch my excitement over my newfound faith.

I was thrilled about my decision to invite God into my life but unsure of what steps to take next. I knew I should read the Bible, go to church and pray, but how was I to go about all of it? What did being a Christian really mean? One day, as I watched my son play soccer, the pastor sauntered up to me.

"Hey, David, just wanted to let you know we are having a Bible class at the church. I think it would be a really great way for you to get involved and learn more about reading the Bible. What do you think?"

The idea excited me, and I agreed to come. The class involved memorizing 81 verses throughout the Bible, and it was intense. But I loved the challenge, and as I learned the verses, I began to understand God's character more. I saw the Bible as more than just a book full of stories — it was God's wonderful message to us. Suddenly, I could not get enough. I wanted to know everything there was about the Christian faith.

To my disappointment, my wife continued to be resistant. She saw my new faith as a threat and could not understand why I'd chosen to give my life up to God when things had been going smoothly for us. I began to lose heart, wondering if there was any hope left for us. I thought of the priest's words when he'd married us: "You two will have lots of problems." Were we really that incompatible? I didn't want to believe that we were. I strongly believed in family, and the idea of divorce was abhorrent. Plus, the last thing I wanted to do was see our family broken in two as my family had been when I was a child.

A year after I invited God into my life, my wife called and dropped a bombshell on me. But it was not a bombshell I'd ever expected in my wildest dreams.

"Your brother wrote a letter. He says he has decided to live the rest of his life as 'Lauren.' He is a woman now."

Nothing could have prepared me for these words. *My brother? Surely, there must be some mistake!* My brother had been an amazing basketball player, an all-star athlete. He'd put himself through college with sports and had made a successful life for himself. I'd been his best man at his wedding. He now had a beautiful wife and made great money. He was the epitome of the all-American family guy. How could this be happening?

Confused and hurt, I called my brother, searching for answers. "Is it true? Why are you doing this?" I cried. "I thought we had an unspoken oath that we would never do this to our kids, that we would never destroy our families."

"You might have had that, but I never did," he replied quietly. "I'm sorry, David, but this is your problem to figure out, not mine."

I remained shocked by his decision. I could not picture my masculine brother as a woman. Shaken and confused, I asked my father what he thought.

"He can do whatever he wants," my father replied nonchalantly.

Inside, I began to slowly come undone. I was so excited about my new faith, but in the past year, not only had my marriage begun to unravel, but my brother had let me down as well. People seemed to be failing me right and left. Everything I'd thought was secure was now shaky. What could I believe in anymore? I knew I had God, but what about the people in my life?

I went to counseling, explaining during the session that I felt lost. Not long after, I picked up a book called *Wild at Heart* by John Eldredge. In it, the author described how every young man will model masculinity from someone in his life.

As I read it, a light bulb went on in my mind. I realized that after my father had walked out on us, my brother had become a father figure of sorts. He'd been my role model for years, and I'd always hoped my life would turn out half as great as his. Now, the one person I'd looked up to since I was a kid had drastically let me down. Accepting his decision was difficult. He was my brother, after all, and I still loved him deeply. But would our relationship ever be the same again?

As I grappled for answers, a guy at church suggested I begin reading the book of Proverbs in the Bible. "It's packed with all sorts of wisdom," he told me. "If you're feeling lost and confused, it's a great place to start."

I did as he said and continued to pore over my Bible. I knew it contained all the answers I needed when life didn't make sense. But I was also learning that being a Christian did not mean I was now immune to life's troubles. If anything, more strife had entered my life since I first set foot in church. I needed to cling to God more than ever, as he was the only sure thing amidst uncertainty.

While the church I was attending provided a good base for my faith, I still longed to see more creativity there. I made several suggestions to the pastor, but he politely turned them down.

"We don't do that here," he said.

Not long after, I attended a funeral for a young athlete on my son's football team whose heart had stopped after jumping off the diving board at a community pool. A large group gathered together to support the family as they grieved, and the pastor of their church presented a wonderful message, inviting anyone who wanted to invite God into his or her life to come forward.

As I observed the community coming together, I realized, *Perhaps it's time to switch churches. I really want to grow and use my gifts to help others, and I'm not sure I can do that where I'm at.*

I found another church to attend, and the congregation welcomed me and my talents with open arms. I joined the creative services team, worked on video production and fundraising and eventually led a songwriter's group.

It felt good to use the gifts God had given me, and I enjoyed being a part of something meaningful. Inspired by the work God was doing through me, I wrote a song called "How Much More."

# Resound

*Take the sum of all I am*
*All I'd ever be*
*Everything I'd hoped for*
*All my plans and dreams*
*Everything from this day forward*
*To you I could decree*
*Yet how much more*
*You have given me.*

*Saved me from this life that ends in death*
*Your eternal breath fills me, Lord*
*Unconstrained, no fear, no pain, no death*
*Your eternal breadth surrounds me*
*It's found me.*
*I stand at the door*
*With gratitude and awe*
*At how much more*
*You have given me.*

The words came straight from my heart, as I realized that playing music wasn't about me. I wasn't the center of the spotlight — God was. And the moment I let myself go and played completely for him, beautiful transformation began to take place. And awesome things began to happen inside of me and at the church.

"I don't just want to play music," I told my team members. "I want to do something with a purpose."

Our team decided to put on a fundraiser concert to benefit missions work. Many of the songwriters were going on a trip to Kenya, and we would be able to draw inspiration from the work that God was doing there. The concert would include video, food, dance, music and, of course, a special message. A few naysayers became skeptical of how we would pull off such a large production, but I remained confident it would be a success. I firmly believed God had told me he would bless the concert.

The night before the big concert, our team rehearsed the musical pieces over and over. The rehearsal went anything but smoothly. We played offbeat, sang off tune and couldn't seem to come together. The entire night was a train wreck. I went home feeling defeated, wondering how on earth things could come together the next day. What if the whole show was a disaster?

Once again, God reminded me that the show was not about me — it was about him. If I gave it fully up to him, he would bless it. It did not matter how many people showed up or how well we played. If he was in it, it would all work out.

To my delight, everything went smoothly and fell into place the next day. All of my worries quickly disappeared as the team began to play together on stage. God ironed out every last detail to perfection, just the way he wanted it.

I shared a story with the crowd about God's excellence, and they listened intently. Afterward, a mother and daughter walked up to me with tears in their eyes.

"My husband just left us," the woman said quietly.

"Your message really spoke to my heart. God is still good, and I have to trust in him. Thank you."

I thanked God that he had used me to reach this hurting woman. I knew there were many more untold stories in the crowd — tragedies and wounds people carried in their hearts. I knew how it felt to carry so much hurt, because I had done so for years after my father walked out of my life. I still struggled with my brother's decision and my wife's resistance toward God. But at last, I understood God's goodness, and I believed he was working in my life. I didn't have everything figured out, but I did have something I hadn't had before — hope.

Things remained tense at home. My wife and I fought often, but I still prayed, asking God to restore our relationship. I didn't want to give up. We had two children and a good life. I focused on work, church ministry and the kids. I loved watching my son thrive in various sports and enjoyed spending time with my daughter, too. Every night, I tucked her in, and we read books, laughed and ended our time with a prayer. We shared a similar sense of humor, and I cherished our special time together.

When she was just 8 years old, I said, "I'm going to have you sign an agreement that reads: 'I, Isabelle, will let my dad tuck me in until I am 18 years old.'"

"Okay," she agreed, giggling.

I hoped we would always be close. My children were the bright spot in our often-tumultuous home. I continued to read my Bible, but my wife rolled her eyes when she saw it in my lap. One day, she threw it at me in disgust. I watched Christian teachers on TV, but she mocked those as well. *God, help me,* I prayed. *I really don't know what to do.*

My wife agreed to come to church with me one Sunday morning. But during worship, she grew furious. She got out of her seat and fell down in the aisle, then stood up and stormed out of the room. I continued worshipping, but my heart sank once again. I could not make her believe in God. Only God could do that. I'd never given up hope that she would accept him into her life, but defeat was slowly encroaching.

In 2005, I stepped away from church involvement. As much as I loved the music ministry, I knew I needed to be on the receiving end, too. It was time to sit back and spend time with God one-on-one. I spent the next few years giving what effort I had left to my marital relationship, still hoping for a miracle. But in 2012, my wife declared she'd had enough.

"I've decided to move out," my wife told me, describing the place she'd be moving into.

Her words were a freight train, plowing me over at 100 miles per hour. They were Niagara Falls, crushing me from head to toe. I had feared this day might come but hoped it wouldn't. I still believed in family and wanted to work things out. I'd married her because I thought she shared those same values. It seemed unfathomable to spend the rest of our lives apart.

"Why don't we talk?" I sputtered, desperate to see her stay.

But my wife didn't want to talk. She packed her things and moved out, leaving a gaping hole in our once-happy home.

I was heartbroken and torn about what to do next. My son had already moved out on his own, but my daughter still lived at home. Both of them knew our marriage was less than perfect and suspected we'd lost that loving feeling long ago. But having watched my parents divorce when I was a boy, I knew there was never a good time to rip a family apart.

I went to the pastors at church and asked for advice. "I'm really struggling. I know the Bible says that if a spouse who doesn't believe in God wants to leave the other spouse, it's okay to let him or her go. But I take my vows seriously. I really don't want to see this marriage end in failure," I told them with a heavy heart.

The pastors knew I'd ridden an emotional roller coaster for a few years. They'd been praying for me and for my wife, hoping along with me that she would accept God into her heart. But even they seemed surprised that I still struggled with whether or not to divorce her. It was obvious my wife had clearly made her choice, and now it was time to grieve and move on.

I continued to mourn the relationship over the next few months. I stayed up late at night, watching the news on TV, hoping sleep would finally beckon and whisk me out of my misery. My daughter, now a teenager, had a life of her own and was not often home. The days grew long and lonely, and I wondered how I'd ever climb out of my pit of sadness. I read my Bible and prayed, but the hole in my heart remained.

One night, I glanced over at my guitar, and it suddenly hit me. *I should start playing the guitar again.* It had been a while since I'd picked it up, but like a good friend I hadn't seen in a while, I missed it. I reached for the guitar and slowly began to strum. And as I did, a happiness I hadn't felt in a long time filled my soul. I kept on playing, pouring my heart into the music as my fingers ran over the strings.

I thought of the many times I'd played with my friend when I was a young man — how the music had brought me so much joy. I remembered my times on stage at church, playing for God as he used me to reach others. My life had not always been easy, but God had always used music to bring healing, joy and fulfillment. As I continued to play that night, God gave me a song of hope. And for the first time since my wife walked out the door, I believed I would be okay.

Forgiveness and recovery came after the mourning. Just as with the death of a loved one, I had to grieve my wife. I had to accept that she was never going to walk back through those doors. I had to grieve the life we'd had together — the good and the bad. I then had to forgive her, remembering that Jesus had forgiven me for the wrong things I'd done when he gave up his life on the cross. Forgiveness was not easy, but with God's help, it was possible. Recovery came next. Wounds take time to heal, and I knew mine would not fully heal overnight. The process was slow and often painful, but I was not alone. I had God by my side, and I had my guitar. I had the songs he'd put in my heart, and during the darkest moments, they played over and over in my mind.

We decided to sell the house and go through with the divorce. Our all-American dream came crashing down as the attorneys handed us papers and the realtor showed up. *This is really happening,* I thought sadly as I glanced around my home. I thought of the many nights I'd tucked my daughter in, laughing together as we shared our secret jokes. I thought of the family dinners around the table, the soccer games, the other memories. Would I ever live and laugh again?

"You should start dating again," my friends suggested.

But I could not imagine dating. I felt like a truck had run me over. How does one hop up and jump back into the dating arena after being plowed over by a truck?

And then, in early 2013, I met someone. I wasn't looking for a relationship at all. She simply drifted into my life, and we clicked from day one. We called each other at 7 p.m. every night, and the next thing I knew, the clock read 11 p.m. The hours flew by like seconds. We shared much in common. But most importantly, we shared a common faith. For the first time, I was able to discuss my faith in God freely with a woman. I didn't have to hide my Bible anymore or pray in silence. At last, I had someone to pray with.

We didn't date. Instead, we simply struck up a beautiful friendship. Though I was truly drawn to her, I also knew my wounds were fresh. If things were meant to be, they would work out in time. For now, I would enjoy the gift of a relationship God had given me after all I'd endured.

On April 19, 2013, I headed to the Conestoga Recreation & Aquatic Center around 4:30 p.m. to work out for a bit. I hopped on the treadmill and began running at a steady pace. Though now in my early 50s, I was always mistaken for being years younger. I tried to stay in shape and remain as active as possible. And staying busy helped take my mind off the stressors of life.

The next thing I knew, I was waking up in a hospital bed.

I rubbed my eyes groggily, trying to figure out where I was. Tubes protruded from my body everywhere, and nearby, a machine beeped. *A hospital? What on earth happened? How did I get here?*

"Your heart stopped beating. You underwent an emergency quadruple bypass surgery," the doctor explained. "You had an occluded artery ventricle … it was totally packed. Probably a genetic thing. You are lucky to be alive. There was an 8 percent chance of survival."

*Quadruple bypass surgery? Surely, there must be some mistake!* I was the picture of perfect health. I worked out regularly at the rec center and had felt great when I'd hopped on the treadmill that afternoon. How could I, of all people, have had a heart attack?

I thanked God that he had spared my life. Shuddering, I realized how close I'd come to not making it. My heart stopped beating. *I should not be here right now. I should be dead,* I realized, incredulous. But who were the angels who had brought me back to life? I had to find out.

Ten days after the surgery, I returned to the Conestoga Recreation & Aquatic Center to piece together the events. A female gym member had been the only other person in the workout room when I'd fallen off the treadmill. My lips had turned blue, and she'd gone for help. Another woman had responded and called to the receptionist to gather the others. The office tech had then called 911.

Everyone jumped into action at once. The aquatic program coordinator initiated CPR, alternating with a nearby lifeguard. Meanwhile, the recreation program coordinator sent another supervisor for the automated external defibrillator, and the receptionist raced to the workout room to make sure it was safe to use. The paramedics then arrived and rushed me to the hospital. When the doctors had asked me my name, I'd apparently responded. They'd then ushered me into surgery. According to all accounts, I was very fortunate to be alive. Timing had been everything — if the employees and gym members had not been equipped or acted as quickly as they had, I would have surely died.

I processed the events over the next few weeks, moving from shock to gratitude. My new friend told me she'd grown concerned when she didn't hear from me by 6:30 p.m. that night. It was through my son's frantic Facebook post at 6 a.m. the following morning that she learned I'd had a heart attack. She immediately went to her friends at

# Alive Again

Resound Church and asked them to pray for me. And God had heard their fervent prayers.

I praised God, thanking him for saving my life. He had shown great care and favor by bringing me back to life and giving me a second chance. Up until that fateful day, I'd believed I was a failure because of my divorce. I felt unworthy of God's love, convinced that my junk was too much for God to handle. I'd sung many songs about his love over the years and even reminded others that God loved them. But it had taken a near-death experience for me to realize that I didn't need to *do* anything to earn that love. And now, I knew it in my heart — God loved me just as I was. The idea was amazingly, perfectly beautiful.

I read my Bible in a new light, stopping at a particularly meaningful passage in Psalm 91: "Whoever dwells in the shelter of the Most High will rest in the shadow of the Almighty. I will say of the Lord, 'He is my refuge and my fortress, my God, in whom I trust'… If you say, 'The Lord is my refuge,' and you make the Most High your dwelling, no harm will overtake you, no disaster will come near your tent. For he will command his angels concerning you to guard you in all your ways. They will lift you up in their hands so that you will not strike your foot against a stone … 'Because he loves me,' says the Lord, 'I will rescue him. I will protect him, for he acknowledges my name.'"

God had done just that for me. He had commanded his angels to guard me. He had rescued me and protected me. I took great comfort in knowing the God who had created the universe cared so much for me. I could rest in his love, knowing he had me safe in his arms. His angels were looking over me.

"You have a new heart and new DNA," my friend told me.

I knew she was right. Not only did I have a new physical heart, but I had a new heart in Christ as well. My life would never be the same again.

❧❧❧

"Today is all about you. I was just on the conveyor belt, passed from capable hands to capable hands." I stood before the group of employees at the Conestoga Recreation Center, happy to thank each one of them for saving my life. "There simply aren't words to describe my gratitude."

It was a beautiful July morning, and the Tualatin Valley Fire and Rescue had decided to honor the employees of the rec center with a short ceremony, recognizing each one of them for saving my life. The TV news reporters showed up as well to document the special day.

As I glanced around me, my heart warmed. Just months earlier, each of these people had been nothing more than strangers or mere acquaintances. But today, I considered them my friends. Each of them had played an integral part in saving my life, and I could not thank them enough.

# Alive Again

"I hope I am seen as living proof that the cost and legal hurdles attached to putting a defibrillator in a public place is worth it. These things are like crosses on the highway — signs that a tragedy once occurred here," I told the crowd.

I then presented the recreation center with several matted pictures resembling a small funeral card. Below my picture were the words: *David Stone: Born October 10, 1960, shocked back to life April 19, 2013.* I also included the meaningful Bible verse Psalm 91, which I read aloud to everyone.

"I am a person of faith," I told the TV cameras and crowd boldly. "I read my Bible every day. And I know that there were most definitely angels in my life." I smiled, nodding my head toward each one of my miracle workers.

As the ceremony ended and I headed home, I thanked God again for his goodness. Since my near-death experience, I viewed the Bible, God and life in a completely new light. I'd always imagined God as an old guy with a beard, grumpy and unapproachable. But I now saw him as full of life and love, perhaps even youthful and adventurous. Over the years, I'd hung on to the belief that I needed to follow a list of "do's and don'ts" for God to be pleased with me. I'd beaten myself up time and time again over my failed marriage, worried I'd missed the mark. But the Bible talked of many men who simply walked with God, engaging in a living relationship with him. Though they tried to impress him with sacrifices and rituals, God repeatedly reminded them that he was not interested in those things. It was their heart and their obedience he was after. At last, I finally understood that I did not need to do anything but readily accept his love.

After my heart attack, I'd begun attending Resound Church with my new friend. After trying several churches since inviting God into my life, I'd finally found a place to call home. I loved the casual atmosphere, friendly faces and grace-filled message the pastor shared every week. He reminded us every week that God was in the business of restoring lives and that we could approach our heavenly father freely no matter where we were and receive his abundant love. Resound offered a place for me to learn, grow and also share the talents God had given me. It felt great to find such a welcoming place to belong.

Learning to give grace to myself continued to be a process for me. Because I was human, I knew I'd continue to make mistakes every day. Just because I was now a Christian did not mean I would not get angry or discouraged at times. I had not "arrived," but I now understood that even when I did mess up, I could simply come to God with my brokenness, and he would embrace me and set me back on my feet. As I reflected on my marriage, I realized that my wife, too, was human. She had come into the marriage bearing her own set of past hurts, as we all do. Until God had opened my eyes to his love, I hadn't paid much attention to him. My wife's eyes had simply not been opened to God's amazing love for her. But that did not mean there wouldn't be a day down the road when she'd embrace him, too. I prayed that one day she'd see that it was not religion that had destroyed our marriage, as she'd once believed, but that it was her own hurting heart. Until then, I could only extend her the same grace I wanted others to extend to me.

As I grew closer to God, he helped me restore my relationship with my older brother. God had helped me embrace my older brother, despite his difficult decision, and our relationship was now better than it had been in years.

One evening, my older brother, who was now my sister, called me up. "You've just been through this miraculous experience. What are the lessons you've taken away from it?" she asked.

"Well, I now fully understand God's love and grace," I explained to her. "I know I've made lots of mistakes over my life, but the cool thing is, God doesn't see any of those. He only sees who he has made me to be through his abundant love. He loves you, too. You can experience the healing that comes through having a faith in Jesus Christ."

My sister was receptive to the words. Since contracting Parkinson's disease, her health had rapidly declined. I knew she contemplated death and now sought deeper meaning in her life. Before we hung up the phone, we promised to talk again soon.

I grew excited as I mulled over our conversation. As a young boy, I'd asked my brother about death, and he'd given a troubling answer. But now, I sensed a stirring in my sister's heart, and I prayed she would invite Jesus into her life before she faced death head on. I recalled the wonderful verse, Romans 8:38-39: "For I am convinced that neither death nor life, neither angels nor demons, neither the present nor the future, nor any powers, neither height nor depth, nor anything else in all creation, will be able to separate us from the love of God that is in Christ Jesus our Lord."

There was nothing that could separate us from God's great love. I now knew what lay on the other side of this earth, and the answer filled me with hope and joy. I only hoped my sister would find that one day soon as well.

My son, who'd claimed seeing me in the hospital was "reality changing," now exchanged "I love you's" with me more often. And though I did not know where my relationship with my new friend would lead, I was grateful to open up my heart again.

With the summer sun hanging over the Oregon sky, I headed home full of joy. *Perhaps I'll go kayaking tomorrow,* I decided. *There's no reason not to enjoy life, after all.* The future remained uncertain, but the possibilities for new opportunities were endless. Perhaps I'd play my music again for a crowd someday. The idea excited me. But even if I never took the stage again, I knew I'd be okay. God had given me a fresh perspective and a new song in my heart. And I was happy to be alive again.

# Beauty for Ashes
## The Story of Nina
### Written by Marty Minchin

"Do you have any family?"

I gave a mostly honest answer. "No."

The social worker stopped scribbling on her pad and looked up at me.

Because I was the only runaway in the halfway house, finding someone to claim me was a priority. The building was populated with a motley collection of juvenile delinquents who were in trouble for everything from gang activity to drugs.

"I don't have a mother," I told the social worker. That was true. She had left me with my father when I was a baby and moved to Israel.

"I ran away from my dad." Contacting him was out of the question.

My grandfather lived only an hour away in Albuquerque, but he was on disability and wasn't fit to care for a teenager. My dad had some family in Texas, but at the time I didn't even think to mention them.

The social worker's only choice was to admit me into the house, and she led me to my room. I heaved my giant duffle bag onto my new bed and smiled. Better days were ahead.

Living in the halfway house was like a breath of fresh air.

# Resound

I ate three meals a day.

Someone drove me to and from school.

When I took a shower, I didn't have to worry about my dad coming into the bathroom to look at me.

I smoked all of the cigarettes I wanted, and I whiled away my extra time playing basketball with my fellow juvies on the halfway house court.

It took the social worker two weeks to locate a relative. When my aunt called me at the halfway house, I was shocked.

Truly, I didn't think anyone would notice that I had gone.

৯৯৯৯

My parents met in Phoenix, Arizona, when my dad was in his early 20s. He was a rock and rolling guitar player, and they ran into each other on the party circuit. My mom was 19 and already the mother of two children. When she got pregnant with me, my parents married quickly and divorced just as fast. Before I was a year old, my mom took off. My half-siblings moved in with their father, and my dad took over with me. My mother insisted that she needed to go on some kind of spiritual quest that required her to move to Israel.

Dad and I flew to Santa Fe, where I spent 12 years staying out of the way of Dad's rotation of girlfriends and endless appetite for drinking and sex.

His drinking started when I was young, and at first it

was mild. The bigger problem was Linda, his new wife, and her awful son, Sylar.

Dad and Linda had a daughter, Maddie, after they got married. I was 3 when Maddie was born. When they went out, which was often, Sylar would babysit us. Sylar was about 10 years old, and he was an angry kid who didn't get along with my dad. Everything that made Sylar angry, Sylar took out on me. It started with threats, kicks and punches, but as we got a little older, his abuse took a crueler turn.

I shared a room with Maddie, who Sylar loved. During a rare interlude when Sylar was being nice to me, I was eager to do anything to earn his affection. He tiptoed into our room one night and asked me to follow him into the living room.

I jumped out of bed and trailed behind him, thinking he wanted to hang out with me. We padded through the pitch-dark house; everyone else was asleep.

Sylar sat on the couch, and all of a sudden, he was completely nude. He asked me to touch him.

I froze.

"No way!" Horrified, I ran back to my room.

Sylar ramped up his abuse in the days that followed, angered by my rejection. Sometimes he would try to get me to eat droppings from our rabbit or drink his urine; it happened one time, and I ended up vomiting it up in the toilet. He called me names while pounding into my ears how much he loved Maddie and hated me.

Anytime my dad left the house, tears involuntarily

poured out of my eyes. I knew no peace from Sylar.

Inevitably, Dad cheated on Linda. Like her son, she turned her rage on me. She'd throw things at me and put me in timeout for hours. Often, she'd direct me into a corner where I'd stand for three or four hours, picking at the sealant and the paint where the drywall met. I got in trouble for everything. One day Linda threw a glass of water at me at lunch when I told her I wanted something.

Dad and Linda finally divorced, and Linda left with Maddie and Sylar. Their departure offered a temporary reprieve, but life with them was only a precursor for the misery Dad's next conquest brought with her.

❧❧❧

Jackie was in her mid-20s, and she shared her love of alcohol with my dad. She took Linda's place in Dad's bed, now with the added fuel of daily glasses of whiskey.

The thin walls of my room provided the shakiest of barriers between me and the circus that went on across the hall. I was barely in kindergarten, and the era of Jackie exposed me to sights and sounds more appropriate for an R-rated movie. Dad and Jackie drank and fought, fought and drank, and drank and fought. They screamed at each other and got in fistfights. She was perpetually bruised from Dad's blows. At the height of one of their worst fights, Dad shoved Jackie outside and down the porch steps. I found blood on the rocks by the bottom stair the next morning on my way to school.

# Beauty for Ashes

When they weren't brawling, Dad and Jackie were having sex or watching videos of people having sex. While most parents opt to read *Good Housekeeping* or *Sports Illustrated*, my dad stacked *Playboy* and *Hustler* on the coffee table, in the bathroom and in his bedroom. If the sounds of Dad's porn movies weren't drifting through my walls, the sounds of the real thing between him and Jackie were. I could hear everything they did, and I was horrified.

Jackie was perpetually jealous of me, and she went to great lengths to get me into trouble or take away any token of affection from Dad. She confiscated a necklace he gave me, but worse, she tattled to him about things I did — and sometimes didn't do.

Her jealousy and Dad's rage followed me around like an angry cloud. One day Dad called me at a friend's house roaring drunk, demanding that I come home immediately.

I ran home crying until I reached the door, then paused with the uncertainty of what I would face inside.

"So, Jackie tells me that you didn't clean the dishes." Dad narrowed his eyes at me, trying to focus. "Is that true?"

My answer didn't matter. Dad grabbed my arm and pulled me into his room, grabbing the paddle he'd carved with my name on it that hung behind his door. He delivered a vicious spanking and then the follow-up punishment: "You're worthless, Nina, nothing but dirt." I hung my head as his words rained down on me. "Tonight, you'll sleep where the dirt is. Under your bed."

When the sun set, I put on my nightgown, stuffed my

pillow and blanket under my bed and crawled in with them. My shoulders shook as I cried, knocking the bottom of the bed when I turned on my side. As the night rolled in, the quiet evening only made it easier to hear the awful sounds of Dad and Jackie across the hall. Mercifully, I finally fell asleep.

Dad's sexual appetite grew monstrous, and when Jackie was out, he began turning to me. At first, he would call me into his room to nap with him. Starved for affection, I climbed into his bed without a second thought. Despite tolerating everything else Dad had done, this pushed Jackie over the edge.

"What is this?" she screamed at him one afternoon, waving a pair of my underwear that she had found in his bed.

Her angry glare shifted to me.

"How did this get in your dad's room?"

I looked at the ground and lied. "I don't know how that got there."

I hated Jackie. It didn't take her long to put two and two together, and she marched into Dad's room and packed her stuff. Then she walked out, for good.

ৼৼৼ

Dad and I were alone for a short window after Jackie left, but he continued satiating his enormous lust for women and alcohol. He'd pour his first glass of whiskey in the morning and often was wasted for most of the day. Sex was everywhere, regardless of his relationship status.

We lived in a doublewide trailer that also served as Dad's woodworking shop. He was a gifted artist, and he made custom doors and gates. He blocked off his work area with big sheets of plastic, progressively converting more of the rooms into a woodshop. The house was littered with tools and wood scraps and smelled like wood, sawdust and the Jameson Irish whiskey that he loved.

On the days when he didn't have a new woman around, he took the opportunity to lecture me about sex. I was 9.

We'd sit across from each other at the kitchen table, and he'd lean on his elbow as he drunkenly spilled poisonous words into my ears.

"Nina, you're worthless," he'd often begin. "You know your mom left because of you." Sometimes his tangents would go on for hours, until well after midnight. My eyes would droop as I tried to act alert.

"You know where the only thing you have is that's worth anything? Look down. It's between your legs. If you ever want any man to love you, you've got to sleep with him."

That certainly seemed to be how Dad defined love in his relationships.

One night, he called me out of my room to meet the hooker he had brought home.

I gaped in awe at her outfit. She was dressed in a miniskirt, high heels and a red leather jacket, and her long blond hair draped down her back. I looked her up and down so hard that even Dad, in his inebriated state, noticed.

"Hi," the hooker offered. What could a third grader and a hooker possibly have to say to each other?

"Go to your room," Dad ordered. "You're being rude."

I never saw her again.

Megan, however, did stay, for months longer than I would have expected. She answered a personal ad Dad had placed in the newspaper and moved right in. She came from a good home in Ohio, and she didn't drink. Dad backed off the booze a little, but when Megan figured out how bad his problem was, she moved out, taking the calm with her.

Dad nearly met his match with Vera. They started dating when I was 10, and we soon moved in with her. Vera trained horses, and I savored every minute I got to spend at the barn with her.

When she and Dad got into fistfights, Vera would throw punches, too. She acted as a buffer between Dad and me, and if I ever had a mother figure in my life, it was her.

Life at Vera's was unstable, though, and Dad continued to drink and abuse me. They broke up and got back together, and when they were off, Dad and I lived in hotel rooms, sometimes for weeks. His custody of Maddie allowed for weekend visits, and often she'd stay with us Friday through Sunday. Maddie and I shared a bed when she was over, and even with her next to me, I still never knew what to expect from Dad. One weekend night, Dad woke me up with a punch in the face before dragging me out of the room.

"C'mon, Maddie," Dad called, motioning her to follow. He stuffed us in the car along with some of his belongings and drove us to a studio apartment that would be our new home. The small space held a studio for his woodworking shop and a loft with barely enough room for two twin beds. Dad and I shared the apartment's single bathroom.

ৡৡৡ

Since I'd started kindergarten, school had been both a welcome escape and a test of my mettle because I had no support system at home. My fair complexion and light blond hair stood out among the olive-skinned kids of Santa Fe, and my classmates regularly poked fun at my looks. Dad didn't cook, and many of our meals consisted of Raman noodles or cereal. I probably looked like the neglected child of an alcoholic that I was. The bus ride home often was the worst part of the day, as I stared out the window and mentally wagered whether my dad would be drunk when I walked in the door.

One constant in my life was staying up late, though not by choice. Sometimes I'd have to endure Dad's long-winded rants or his molestation. Dad frequently fell behind in his woodworking projects because he drank so much, so he'd work late to catch up. Other times, he would play his guitar until 2 a.m., the music so loud that he might as well have been rehearsing in the corner of my room. In fifth and sixth grade, I grew so fed up with it that I'd grab my blanket and pillow and Dad's keys and trek outside to the car. Even if it was the dead of winter and snowing, sleeping in the car was worth a few more hours of uninterrupted rest.

By seventh grade, I was hardly attending school. On the days I did attend, I'd sleep through class. I'd taken up smoking cigarettes at age 11 because the nicotine eased my anxiety. Dad smoked at least three packs a day, and it was easy to steal cigarettes and butts from him. Stealing and smoking his pot was just as easy. I fell in with a crowd of hoodlums, and school became nothing more than an excuse to get away from my dad for eight hours. Dad never updated the school when we moved around, so the administration didn't know how to contact him to tell him I was absent. I skipped school to hang out and smoke with my friends way more than I attended class. They were the only people in my life who I believed loved me.

At home, Dad became more violent and persistent with his molestation as I grew older. I layered on clothing at night like a shield against his advances, and I stayed on alert, never knowing when he would lash out.

At his worst, Dad punched me in the face, sometimes making my nose bleed. He kicked me in the shins with his cowboy boots and backhanded me across the face. He once threw a two-by-four at my head. I'd go to school with my face bruised, and no one ever said anything.

One night, Dad hustled me up to the loft, with Maddie

watching below, and wrapped a wire coat hanger around my neck.

"I'm doing this because I love you," he slurred. "This is how I show you that I love you."

As with all of Dad's abuse, I took it quietly and didn't fight back. I never screamed. But by middle school, I couldn't absorb any more. Plus, he was getting aggressive with Maddie, who he'd never abused, on her weekend visits. To keep him away from her, I'd try to get his attention so he'd abuse me instead.

કજીકજી

I didn't know much about God. But the night I decided to run away from my dad, I started talking to him.

Dad followed me up into the loft, where I was trying to get in bed. He pulled off my layers of clothes and forced me to perform an act on him. Dad was too drunk to notice or care that I cried through the whole thing.

*God, please set me free. I can't take this anymore.*

When I finished, he pushed me over. He had never completed the act with me, and for the first time I feared he would.

"No, don't," I cried, trying to squirm away.

All of a sudden, he just stopped. He passed out as I crawled into my bed. The tears wouldn't stop, and I cried myself to sleep listening to Dad's drunken breathing just feet away.

*I'm done. I'm not living here another day.*

# Resound

The next morning, as usual, my dad had no recollection of what had happened the night before. He had been too drunk. As I pulled on my clothes and got ready for school, my skin crawled with the memory of what almost happened the night before. I opened the refrigerator door, and as expected there was nothing inside.

"You should cover your face with your hair," Dad suggested, giving my bruised face a pointed look.

*I'll show him. I'll run away and scare the crap out of him. He'll be shocked into sobriety and finally decide that I'm worth more than alcohol.*

I didn't have a long-term plan for running away. After school, I called a friend of mine I'd known since fifth grade and told him my plan. I'd bring my stuff to his house and stay there for a few days. I'd disappear quietly.

I begged my friend not to tell his dad, a local social worker, as I didn't want any adults interfering. That night Dad spent the night with Vera, who he'd gotten back together with for the hundredth time, and I methodically stuffed my clothes in my bag in the loft. For once, the studio apartment felt peaceful. It was like an other-worldly presence was assuring me that it was time to leave.

In my mind, I heard instructions as clear as day: *Pack your bag, and hide it outside under the staircase.*

The next morning was a Saturday, and Dad, who already was drinking at 10 a.m., believed my lie that I was going to spend the day at the library. I lugged my big duffle bag to the bus stop and boarded the public bus, a familiar mode of transportation because I took it to school across town. I got off in downtown Santa Fe and stood awkwardly on the sidewalk. I had no money or real plan, and my friends were at the mall.

A car pulled to a stop in front of me, and my friend's mother called out the open passenger window.

"Hey, what are you doing?" For some reason she didn't remark on the huge bag at my feet. "Do you need a ride to the mall?"

She popped the trunk, and I pushed my bag into it before hopping into the car. I met up with my two best friends in my seventh grade class, Micah and Heather, at the mall after she dropped me off.

Micah, ever the son of a social worker, jumped to action.

"I'm going to call my dad."

"NO." I didn't need to involve him. "I'm just going to stay with you for a few days."

He wasn't interested in my amateur plan, and he marched over to a payphone and filed an abuse claim against my dad with the State of New Mexico. Then he called his dad and held out the receiver to me.

"Talk to him," he ordered.

Now crying, I reluctantly put the phone to my ear.

"What's going on with your dad?" a kind voice asked.

Micah's dad picked us up a few hours later and drove us to the Department of Social Services. Throughout the 12 years of abuse, I had only told Micah and Heather what had happened. It was time my story had a wider audience.

# Resound

I spent the afternoon in a conference room eating pizza, while the State took custody away from my father.

❧❧❧

The halfway house was designed for kids who were in between juvenile hall and living on the street, but I was there for protective custody because the State had nowhere else to send me. I told them I had no family to call.

For two weeks, I enjoyed a sort of vacation. At my dad's, I had to do all the cleaning, dish washing and laundry. I rode public transportation to school, and I rarely got a good night's sleep. At the halfway house, I was well fed, well rested and free from the fear of what my dad would do next.

When Dad showed up at Aunt Sharon's door in Texas the day after he lost custody of me, she didn't believe his story that I was staying with a friend. She started calling around and after a few days found me at the halfway house.

"Nina, what's going on?" Her voice was frantic.

I told her the summary, but she already knew some of it because she had talked with social workers before she got to me.

"Your dad came to see us."

I was shocked that my dad had been so upset by my disappearance that he sought out rarely seen family a state over. The whole family now knew that my 30 days in the halfway house were almost up, and nothing was standing between me and the foster care system.

Suddenly, the family I had always wanted came out of the woodwork. My grandfather had my aunt from Alabama drive him over from Albuquerque. An aunt I had never met flew in from Alabama and wanted to adopt me. I told the social worker that the family I really wanted to live with was my Aunt Peggy and Uncle Ted, who lived in Phoenix and were the only relatives I really had ever spent any time with. Their family, with four kids and a stable home, sounded like heaven.

They called me at the halfway house to talk about our future. Uncle Ted, who worked for Intel, had just accepted a job as a project manager for the company in Israel, and the family was packing to move to the Middle East that summer.

"Nina, we don't know what to do," Uncle Ted said as we both cried.

"I really want to live with you guys. I don't know anyone else."

Uncle Ted cut through the agony of the situation with a quick decision. "Okay. We're coming."

Thirty-eight hours before the State initiated foster-care proceedings, Aunt Peggy loaded her kids into her car and drove to Santa Fe. She sat down with me to lay a few ground rules before she would agree to adopt me.

"No dating until you're 16," she said. "You do your homework and follow the rules, and you can live with me."

That was easy. "Okay," I agreed.

Aunt Peggy met with a judge, walked into the courthouse and signed adoption papers within a few hours.

Dad showed up at the custody hearing, but I didn't have to attend because the State had recorded my testimony. I submitted a letter expressing my deep desire to live with my aunt and uncle, which the judge read. The attorney told my aunt he had never seen custody signed over so fast in his 25 years of experience. My aunt called it a miracle.

Dad lost permanent custody, and Aunt Peggy drove me and my cousins back to Phoenix. I finished seventh grade there, and that summer we moved to Israel.

❧❧❧

In the Bible, the historical account of the ancient Israelites, the people God chose to be his followers, describes how God led them into a beautiful and bountiful land after 40 years of wandering in a desert. Thousands of years later, I found myself delivered from a desert into my own "promised land" in Israel.

No one knew me or my past in Israel. For the first time in my life, I could be a kid. In Santa Fe, I had a sense that my life was playing out on a movie screen and that everyone was watching but not doing anything. In Israel, I was surrounded by friends, teachers and family who cared about me. I attended an outstanding private school, and my teachers were interested in my education. My grades soared. I played sports and traveled. Living in the land where Christianity began, I began to feel that God was around me. I didn't know much about God, but now I felt him closer than I ever had.

After a year in a gated community, we moved much closer to our school. Our new town, Herzalia, was the Hollywood of Israel. The beach was a five-minute walk, and our friends lived all around. Our social world opened up, and my cousin Frank and I basked in the freedom of being teenagers living in a foreign country. We spent hours drinking and smoking on the beach, meandering through our carefree lives with our pack of friends. I dated some guys and messed around with them, but I never had sex. My childhood trauma lingered too close.

The day came when Uncle Ted announced that he was being transferred back to the United States. He and Aunt Peggy were separating, and she would stay in Israel. The kids would live with Uncle Ted in Portland because he was the parent with a job.

The week after our school year ended, when I was 16, we flew back to the States and moved into Uncle Ted's house in Beaverton, Oregon. Israel had been an instant reprieve from my childhood, and I basked in my new life there rather than dealing with my past. Returning to the States forced me to confront it, piece by piece.

Israeli teenagers were pretty chaste, but in Beaverton it seemed like everyone at my high school was having sex or talking about it. I dated disgusting guys and lost my virginity when I was 17. I dated my first serious boyfriend, Mac, for about a year, and all we did was have sex. My dad's rambling treaties on my worth played out, as I began to live like I believed that guys only liked me for sex. I seemed be a magnet for men who had sex on the brain.

After thriving academically in Israel, I barely graduated from high school. I fell into a depression and hardly participated in school, doing just enough to get by. After a year of nightmarish fights and breaking up and getting back together with Mac, he dumped me to go out with my friend. I had no tools for handling the abandonment issues that had festered in me since my mom left.

Chronic depression had given birth to insomnia during my two years of high school in Beaverton, and I had a supply of Trazodone on hand for those nights I couldn't sleep. One afternoon I downed a handful of pills, laid down on my bed and hoped I'd never wake up again.

Sleep didn't come as quickly as I'd thought. I didn't drift off for 45 minutes, and then people kept coming in and out of my room and waking me up. I'd dropped Trazodone pills on the floor, and the empty bottle was in plain sight. I wasn't trying to hide anything. I was desperate for peace and a release from the ever-present hurt that tormented me.

When my uncle got home from work, I was awake, but my body was almost frozen with paralysis. Hardly able to move or walk, I began hallucinating. Somehow I dragged myself to my uncle and told him what I had done.

"I think I'm sick," I mumbled. I told him I had taken the pills and wasn't sure what to do. I felt awful, and fear and paralysis were creeping over me. I perched on the edge of his bed while he looked up information on poison control online.

"Nina, why would you do this?" I had put Uncle Ted through so much. When he found out I was having sex, he'd had to put me on birth control pills. We'd have loud arguments, and I'd scream at him in frustration.

Uncle Ted determined that I needed to go to the hospital. As I slumped into the car, I could feel my body shutting down.

"Why did you do this?" he repeated, looking over at me as we drove. I didn't have a good answer, but my broken heart knew that it was because I didn't see any reason why I shouldn't.

I passed out on the hospital couch, while Uncle Ted tried to answer the doctor's questions about what I had taken and why. The hospital sent me home, and I slept for 14 hours. I upset Uncle Ted so much that he still won't talk about the incident.

అఁఁఁ

Uncle Ted had promised me and my cousins that if we graduated from high school, he'd buy us a plane ticket to wherever we wanted. I chose London, and I spent three weeks there with a friend. We drank a lot and smoked pot, which I justified with God by reminding myself that it was a plant that grew out of the earth, not some unnatural substance.

The vacation from life in Oregon helped me muster up the strength to break it off once and for all with Mac, who still came around sometimes. That opened the door for Eric, who was hanging around my house with my cousin Frank when I returned from Europe.

I'd known Eric from Shakespeare class in high school, but I'd hardly noticed when he'd dropped out of school because he was a meth addict. He was a jerk and definitely weird, but when he took a liking to me that summer, I felt a strange attraction between us. I was eccentric myself, and something between us clicked.

Now that I was a legal adult, Uncle Ted decided he'd had enough. I had just turned 18, had quit my hostess job at Chevy's, a Tex-Mex restaurant in town, and was dating a sketchy guy. Eric, who'd bought me a half a gallon of tequila for my 18th birthday, was prone to disappearing, sometimes for a week or more. I'd sit around waiting for him to come back, even though I had no idea where he was or who he was with.

Uncle Ted sat me down and told me he didn't want me to live at his house anymore. I handled the news by smoking a bowl with a friend, letting the smoke blur the reality that I had no job, no money, no ambition and nowhere to live.

To add to my misery, Eric suddenly found God and broke up with me to pursue a new "righteous" lifestyle. His mom had started taking him to a group of Christians in Portland who had a powerful connection with God. Volunteers at their organization would place their hands on visitors and talk to God for them, asking for God to heal them and give them freedom from the things that hurt them.

When Eric told me that he was breaking up with me because he had become a Christian, I had no concept of what that meant. In my mind, our relationship was too intense and intertwined to simply part ways over religion. He was being an idiot, and I just needed to get his attention and push sex on him more. It worked.

Eric lived six blocks from Uncle Ted, so it was not uncommon to run into him around the neighborhood. One week before my eviction date from Uncle Ted's, he found me sitting in a car with a friend, smoking pot. He tapped on the window to get my attention.

"I can't hang out tonight because my mom is taking me to that Christian group again."

I was stoned out of my mind, but a question surfaced amid the haze.

"Who is Jesus?" I stared at Eric through the open car window. "Is it true you have to believe in him to be a Christian?"

"Yes," Eric replied. "The foundation of Christianity is Jesus Christ."

"Huh. Why don't you take me with you today?" I had no idea what this place was or who these Christian people were, but I knew that my boyfriend was going to do something without me. I was jealous of his time.

# Resound

His mom drove us there, where she and Eric were enrolled in a training class for people who wanted to volunteer. I followed Eric and his mom into the classroom.

I didn't fit in. Looking like the resident punk, my tongue, nose and ears were pierced, and I had on a miniskirt and a low-cut top that barely contained my cleavage. And I was stoned.

I settled into a chair and listened to an hour of the group's leader, Vicki, talk about crazy stuff. She covered angels, prayer and something called "spiritual warfare," while I zoned out.

Afterward, Eric introduced me to Vicki.

"This is my girlfriend, Nina." Vicki smiled from ear to ear.

"We've heard so much about you." I was amazed by how friendly Vicki was, despite my appearance and obvious state of mind. When she asked if she could pray for me, I readily accepted. No one had ever asked to pray for me before.

I followed Vicki up a set of crooked stairs into a hallway of empty bedrooms above the Korean church where the meeting had been held. Four or five people were waiting, and I balked. This felt like a trap.

I sat down, anyway, and lowered my head. The volunteers laid their hands on me and began to talk to God. Their voices surrounded me with peace and confidence. Suddenly, I broke. Whatever evil force had held a stronghold on my life for all those years had lost its grip. The volunteers saw my tears and sensed the rapid changes stirring in my soul.

"Do you want to accept Jesus as your Lord and Savior?" one asked me joyfully.

I had no idea who Jesus was. "Yes!" I shouted.

A celebration broke out in the room, as the volunteers clapped and laughed with happiness. Something supernatural had happened inside me, and the room swirled with the prayers of the volunteers as they talked to God for another hour. A window had opened into my soul, and God was pouring into it through the words of these people. In the emotion and chaos, one message from God crystallized in my heart: He loved me.

လလလ

A world that had once been tinged with gray and brown was now vibrant with color. My spirit became sensitive to the drugs and other vices that were regular parts of my life, and I needed to get away from them. Uncle Ted wouldn't budge on my eviction date, so Eric's mom offered me a bedroom across the hall from Eric. It's hard to go backward once you have an intimate relationship with someone, though, and we were both new in our relationship with God and susceptible to falling back into our old ways. We were going to church with his mom and trying to do the right thing, but we knew our best course of action was to get married, even though we were only teenagers.

# Resound

Eight months after we started dating, Eric and I were married. We moved into a one-bedroom, one-bathroom apartment under Vicki Anderson's house, and she only charged us $300 per month to live there. We did odd jobs, such as yard work, to pay our bills.

When I was 19, I had the terrifying realization that I was pregnant.

We moved back in with Eric's parents after Daniel was born. Eric had a job, and I stayed home with our baby. I had a difficult relationship with Eric's mom, who also was home a lot, so I tended to hibernate in my room with the baby. I rarely ventured out of the house. As the due date of our second son, Paul, drew near, I told Eric that I couldn't live there another day.

Another day turned into five months, but we eventually got our own apartment. I started going to school in Portland after Eric came home from work, taking the MAX from Beaverton to Portland to get to classes. We celebrated our three-year anniversary, marveling that we had made it this far.

Three months later, Eric left a message for me on my computer. He thought we were having "issues."

*I love you,* he wrote, *but I need to take some time away.*

Completely shocked, I sat down to consider what he meant. What kind of issues, other than we were in our early 20s with two little kids finally figuring out how to live on our own?

Eric was gone for several days. I tried calling his cell

phone, but the ringer sounded in our apartment because he'd left the phone. Frantic, I thumbed through the calls on it to figure out where he could be. He had placed a lot of calls to a number I didn't recognize, so I tried it, hoping he'd be with whoever answered. It rang through to a woman's voicemail.

"Hi, it's Nina. I'm looking for my husband, Eric, and I thought he might be with you. I'm home with our two kids. Please have him call me if you're with him."

Eric had left in our car, and I had no money and was freaking out. Where could he be? Why would he take off like that? Finally, a friend from church walked me through the obvious.

"Do you think he could be having an affair?" she gently suggested.

"No, that's not what it is." I had explained away his absence, his note and texts from the strange phone number telling him "I love you" as coming from a good friend.

My friend prodded again. "I think he's having an affair."

Her words suddenly made sense, and the phone, the texts and the disappearance made sense. *My husband was having an affair.*

Eric returned three days after he left. He immediately told me that he wanted a divorce and was seeing Olivia, a girl we'd known in that fateful high school Shakespeare class. They'd run into each other at a coffee shop while I was in class.

# Resound

སྱོཛྱོཛྱོ

Eric departed in spurts. He came and left as he pleased, taking our car and leaving me to care for our little boys. It turned out that he had another cell phone, which is why he left the one I knew about at home so much. Oftentimes, he would swing through the apartment in the middle of the night and drop off food. Otherwise, the boys and I would take public transportation to the grocery store. Sometimes friends would leave bags of food on the doorstep.

I had never learned how to handle my emotions, and I was beside myself with grief. I'd gained a lot of weight during my pregnancy with Paul, and when Eric left I all but stopped eating and lost 40 pounds in three months. If I was awake when Eric made an infrequent visit to our apartment, I tried to woo him with sex. Sometimes it worked.

A friend from church who knew that Eric and I still had sex called me one day with a warning.

"You need to stop sleeping with Eric," he said. "I know you guys are still married, but it is very important that you listen to me. Make sure there is no sexual contact."

I should have heeded his warning. Getting pregnant for the third time was like putting the cherry on top of an already beautifully manifested nightmare.

Like many women, I sensed right when it happened. I drove myself to Planned Parenthood to get a morning-after pill, but they made me take a pregnancy test first. I knew it would be positive, but I was stunned when the nurse told me I was five weeks pregnant. My intuition had been off.

"Do you want to schedule an appointment?" she asked.

I had made a choice, and now I needed to deal with the consequences. I disobeyed God and didn't listen to my friend from church.

"No, I don't want an abortion."

Eric and I had gotten married with the best intentions, trying to make an honorable choice that followed God's law. Now, everything was a disgusting mess. I was having sex with my husband who was trying to leave me for someone else. After I got pregnant but before I started showing, I slept with another man a few times. Eric and I got in a huge fight in the car, and I bit his arm to get him to let go of my cell phone. After an arrest and a jury trial, the assault charges against me were dropped.

With no job and no money, I was evicted from the apartment. Eric moved in with his girlfriend, and Uncle Ted let me and the boys move into his house. Miraculously, an assisted living facility hired me when I was seven months pregnant.

Meanwhile, I prayed and prayed for my marriage. I regularly visited the Christian group in Portland, often dragging the kids with me so that I could pray and talk with the volunteers there. Sometimes I'd stay for hours, letting the Bible verses we read aloud and the prayers slowly heal my wounds. I spent a year crying for my marriage, desperately wanting my relationship to reflect what Jesus taught in the Bible.

My growing belly was a constant concern. How could I possibly work full time and take care of an infant and two young children? My uncle and aunts began to rumble that I should give this baby up for adoption. My aunt in Texas even offered to take him. Eric pushed me to consider it. It seemed like everyone was ganging up against me.

I turned to Mike, my pastor from church, for advice again.

"Nina, when you are standing before the Lord, and God is judging the decisions you made in your life, you will be responsible for this decision, not anyone else. The next time your uncle tells you to give your baby up for adoption, I would encourage you to tell him that you believe God is telling you to keep him."

Thoughts of my mother abandoning me would not leave my mind. How could I keep two children and give the other away?

When David was born, I held him in my arms and wailed, my tears spilling down on his newborn head. Eric and I had acted the part of happy parents on the day of David's birth, but the next day, he went back to his girlfriend, and I was still a 24-year-old single mom with three kids.

I chose my baby's name carefully. "David" means "beloved" in Hebrew, and I wanted him to know that despite the circumstances around his coming into the world, he was loved.

# Beauty for Ashes

৵৵৵

Six years after my divorce, my life has entered a season of quiet. I'm raising three boys on my own in a two-bedroom apartment, driving an old van my uncle gave me after my divorce. Food stamps help me buy enough food for my family, as I don't make enough money at my full-time job at the assisted living center to get by. I haven't fallen in love again. I haven't graduated from the business program I recently started, but I am doing well in my classes.

Ten years into following God, I've grown to know him well. I've worked with college students at church, completed an abuse recovery class for women and traveled to China on a mission trip with my church. I've developed a close group of friends who share my faith in God. When God recently prodded me to take another step in getting to know him better, I found Resound Church. A friend had mentioned the church, and it sounded really cool. The first church service I attended there blew me away. I love sitting in the movie theater where Resound Church holds its Sunday meetings and absorbing the worship music and teachings about God. I believe God has placed me in a season of quietude and reflection, and Resound Church has been the perfect place for me to rest and get ready for my next stage of life. I look forward to getting more involved in the life of this church.

Recently, I pulled my camera out of the closet. When I was 19 and just getting to know God, he had given me a vision, showing me that I would photograph people who were homeless and destitute. My photographs would show that their faces were beautiful because they were people who God had created and loved. In the ensuing chaos of my life, though, I had stored my new camera away.

A few years ago, I began to ask God for direction for my life. He told me that it was time for me to go back to school, and I am now working on a business degree. It will be a long road and a lot of work. God told me it will be worth it.

I've toted the camera to work on occasion, taking pictures of the precious senior citizens I work with. God prompted me to do more. When I asked my Christian friends to talk to God about photography, one of the women saw a picture in her mind of a schoolbook with a heart on it.

*What could this image mean?* I turned it over in my head, searching for symbolism that could guide me.

A friend provided an answer.

"Maybe God is telling you to follow your heart."

"That's it!"

As much as I enjoy working at the assisted living home and would like to pursue a CNA degree, my heart lies with the camera. I want to take pictures of others, so they will see in themselves what God has shown me. The faces in my photographs may not be faces the world considers important, but I hope that the images reveal that God loves and values them, regardless of their looks or status.

## Beauty for Ashes

When I turned the lens on myself, I saw more than just an image in the resulting photographs. The woman in the picture is striking, with a captivating gaze. She stares at the camera with an expression of peace and confidence.

*You are loved, Nina,* God whispers. *Look at your face in the photograph. This is how I see you.*

*Beautiful.*

# Headlock
## The Story of Jordan
### Written by Angela Welch Prusia

*Clink.* The rock my cousin whirled through the air ricocheted off metal. Moonlight did little to illuminate the target.

"Score." Tyler reached for a high five. "Glad you snuck out now?"

I gave a half smile. A stray cat ran across the alley, beady yellow eyes glaring at us.

"Admit it. You'd never have any fun if it weren't for me."

It was true. Nothing exciting happened in Cedar Rapids, Iowa — other than my cousin's mischievous exploits.

I lobbed a rock at nothing in particular.

"Hey, what are you guys doing?" A gruff voice called out from a porch shrouded in shadows.

"Run!" Tyler yelled.

My heart pounded in my chest as we took off in opposite directions. Better to scatter and outrun trouble. We met up later on the Cedar River dike near Tyler's house.

"That dude was scary." Tyler picked up another handful of rocks and threw one into the rushing current. "Did he chase you?"

# Resound

The distinctive whir of propeller blades cut off my response.

*Thump, thump, thump.*

A helicopter hovered above us, spotlighting us in its bright searchlight. Seconds later, two police cruisers blocked any path of escape.

A cop got out of the first vehicle. "We have reports of vandals smashing cars."

Tyler muttered an expletive under his breath. The guy in the alleyway probably reported us.

"I swear we weren't doing nothing," Tyler tried to explain, but the evidence in his hand told another story.

"Why don't you boys take a ride with us?" The cop's partner handcuffed the two of us.

I swallowed the panic threatening to erupt. My parents were going to kill me.

☙☙☙

The ride in the police cruiser made Tyler and me legends to our friends at middle school. My parents, on the other hand, grounded me from my cousin.

Tyler and I were best friends and a dangerous combination. If baseball, football and club wrestling didn't occupy my time, I'd probably be locked away in juvenile detention.

Fall, I played football. From November to March, wrestling season filled my nights with practice and weekends with tournaments. My father breathed sports.

# Headlock

Like other Iowans, he believed the claim that Iowa was "the wrestling capital of the nation." Baseball bridged the rest of the year. Traveling with the team took me all over the Midwest and to faraway places like Cooperstown, New York.

❧❧❧

Mom was one of my biggest fans.

When sports didn't take up my Sundays, I joined Mom at church and even went to church camp a few times in the summer. I didn't really understand what drew my mom to worship a god I couldn't see. She'd become a Christian shortly after marrying my dad, but he wanted nothing to do with her beliefs. He refused to step foot in a church, even when us four kids went to see Mom get baptized.

By middle school, my social life and sports took center stage. I made time for church on Christmas and Easter. Otherwise, I followed in my father's footsteps.

Traveling to weekend wrestling tournaments connected me and my dad. Many weekends, we'd be on the road long before sunup, the smell of Dad's coffee filling the car as we sang country songs together. Though he wasn't big on showing his affection, Dad's favorite song, "A Love Without End" by George Strait, expressed the love a father has for his children.

"That's my boy," I heard my father telling others in the crowd at my tournaments.

# Resound

"Come on, son!" he'd yell from the edge of the wrestling mat. "You can pin him!"

As soon as I came off the mat, Dad would hand me a bottle of water or Gatorade. After meets, we'd stop at McDonald's and relive the matches over Big Macs. Back home, he'd replay the video footage he'd taped of me wrestling, saying, "Jordan can take on anyone."

≈≈≈

When high school started, I capitalized on my older brother's popularity. Jay's friends dubbed me "Little Jay" because we looked so much alike. As a freshman, I knew half the senior class because of my brother's parties.

At one party, music shook the ceiling above me as I watched a movie downstairs with my girlfriend. The television screen flickered in the dark. A few partygoers stumbled into the basement, then danced back toward the keg.

"Sounds like our brothers are having fun." Ashley snuggled into my embrace.

"Jay's a party animal." I grinned. "Want a beer?" I grabbed one of the cans my brother had given me. She took a sip while I chugged mine down. I didn't have much experience with alcohol, but I'd seen enough drinking games. I handled my beer like a pro.

Ashley laughed at me. "You have some on your lip."

She kissed me, and I melted. High school promised to be great.

# Headlock

᯼᯼᯼

Pain shot through me on the football field a few months later.

"Not again." I gritted my teeth and cradled my arm. I'd dislocated my shoulder two years earlier and knew what I faced. The very thought of sitting out the wrestling season as a freshman compounded my pain. My coach expected great things after I'd placed fourth in the state as a club wrestler.

"You have to have surgery." The doctor pronounced my death sentence.

I bit back anger.

"Are there any other options?" my dad asked.

The doctor simply shook his head. "Have the surgery, heal and you'll be as good as new for next season."

*Next season. No!*

Watching my teammates train upset me. I cursed my rotten luck. They improved their wrestling technique while I rotted on the sidelines.

My wrestling friends tried to encourage me, but long weekends taunted me. After wrestling tournaments, I often joined my friends and drowned my misery in alcohol.

Party weekend turned to party weekend turned to party weekend.

I wanted more out of high school than parties, but I told myself I could quit drinking at any time — especially when wrestling started again. Instead, alcohol became a faceless opponent, locking me in moves I couldn't shake. Addiction soon pinned me in a headlock.

હ્ર હ્ર હ્ર

By the time my sophomore wrestling season started, I couldn't wait to get back on the mats. I promised myself I would train harder, work longer and prove to Coach that I had what it took to make it to state wrestling. My plan succeeded the first few weeks. Then Thanksgiving break hit, and I headed to a party with some friends. Minutes after my arrival, the police showed up.

I tested clean when I blew into the Breathalyzer, but the cops still called my parents. Word leaked out to the athletic director, and Coach found out. I got suspended for the next two dual meets and a Saturday tournament.

I kicked myself for letting my teammates down. I hated my new reputation as *that* guy.

હ્ર હ્ર હ્ર

I managed to stay out of trouble the remainder of my sophomore and junior wrestling seasons, but the desire to party only grew stronger. My party friends bragged about weekend beer fests I missed because of wrestling tournaments. In the middle of meets, my mind began to wander to the next party and the next drink. Wrestling friends talked about renting hotel rooms over the weekend of state wrestling if they didn't qualify. My mouth watered over the consolation prize — bathtubs filled with beer.

My training paid off when I made it to semifinals my junior year. I could finally prove my worth as a wrestler.

The announcement came over the sound system for the 152-pound weight class.

Dad took my face in his hands. "Win this for your grandfather."

I swallowed the lump in my throat and took the mat. Even after my grandpa's funeral weeks earlier, I couldn't believe one of my biggest fans would not be in the stands.

My opponent stared at me with steely eyes. He might be taller and more built, but I'd wrestled him before in other meets and won each time. Sweet victory was mine.

I shuffled my feet and got into position. *I've got this match.*

The whistle blew, and we grappled for the advantage. The roar of the crowd sounded like a faint muffle through my headgear. I couldn't let distractions break my focus. Wrestling was already a head game. Pushing down fear and the desire to drink was hard enough.

One minute of the two-minute period ticked away on the clock.

"No!" Dad screamed from the sidelines when my opponent gained a point.

Fans stood to their feet, the tension of our match taking attention away from the other wrestlers on the floor.

I swore to retaliate. This was my match. Time for my signature move — high crotch to a double leg take down.

# Resound

*You're going down.* I lifted my opponent in the air, ready to slam him down on the mat.

The whistle blew.

*Bam.* He hit the mat.

Too late.

The referee grabbed my opponent's hand and lifted it above his head. "We have a winner."

I lost. I was devastated.

చచచ

The loss became my excuse to party. *Why kill myself with training for fourth place? Why sacrifice my weekends if I can't bring home the trophy?*

Coach encouraged me to stay focused. Competition was fierce, and making it to state was prize in itself. "Work hard," he said. "And you'll claim the victory your senior year."

The call of alcohol trumped his pep talk.

Older friends wooed me with their stories of the college party scene. I was burnt out from sports and fueled for fun. I still believed the lie that I could control my drinking. Instead, I found myself drinking to the point of blacking out. I woke up in places I couldn't remember with girls I didn't know.

In sober moments, I stared at myself in the mirror, wondering who I'd become.

చచచ

# Headlock

Not long after I graduated, Tyler and I hung out with friends in his dorm room in Iowa City. I popped the tab on a beer I'd gotten with my fake I.D.

"This is the life." I gulped down the amber liquid. "No more high school. Partying 24/7."

We wrestled around on the floor between more beers.

"You guys hungry?" one of Tyler's friends asked after a couple hours.

"Oh, yeah." I stood on wobbly feet. Four of us made it to the gas station when I stumbled to the ground.

"Give me your arm, Jordan." Tyler helped me up while one of the other guys offered his support. "We need to get you off the street."

I joked around while the two of them dragged me back to the dorms. At the hill in front of the main entrance, I decided I could make it the rest of the way.

"You sure?" Tyler asked.

I faked a stumble and laughed at his reaction. I ran up the last few steps.

"See? I'm a big boy." I gave Tyler a playful push and lost my balance.

"Uggh." I toppled backward down the slope, landing in a heap in front of a campus security guard.

"I'm calling the cops, if you three want to stick around," he warned Tyler and his friends. They disappeared, leaving me alone with the guard. My breath test revealed a level three times the legal limit. The cop cited me with public intoxication and hauled me down to jail.

# Resound

I waved to a friend from the back of the patrol car, oblivious to my situation.

The next morning, I awoke on a thin mattress on the floor of a jail cell. I stared at the orange jumpsuit I wore, wondering how I'd gotten into this mess. I tried to call Tyler, but I couldn't remember his number.

"Okay, ladies," a gruff guard called out to me and my cellmates. "Time to go before the judge."

My head was killing me as I stood in line in front of a television screen where a judge read my charges.

"Do you plead guilty or not guilty?" he asked.

"Not guilty."

The guys behind me laughed.

"You think this is a joke?" The judge frowned.

"No, sir." I realized my mistake. "I meant guilty."

❧❧❧

Guilt and shame began to plague me. I knew there had to be more to life than getting drunk, but I felt lost. I didn't know what career to pursue, so I enrolled in community college and started classes in heating and air conditioning, like my brother. After a semester, I knew the program wasn't for me, so I worked on my general education classes and moved in with my brother.

Jay's house was known as a huge party house. We played so much beer pong, sticky beer residue and mud caked the floor downstairs. Mornings after parties, the neat freak in me cringed at the mess of empty beer cans.

# Headlock

One evening back home with my parents, I took a walk with my mom. Dad and I butted heads over my partying, but Mom never said anything. She prayed for me in the same way she had for my dad. Not only had he stopped drinking, Dad had become a Christian after reading Lee Strobel's *The Case for Christ*. Now he went to church regularly with Mom, and I saw the difference Jesus made in him.

"Help me!" I wanted to yell out loud to her, but the words wouldn't leave my lips. *Could I really change? What would I do on weekends?* My addiction was an opponent I felt I couldn't beat.

❧❧❧

"Your uncle is taking a group of guys to work at a resort this summer," Mom told me not long after our walk. "Why don't you give him a call? It'd be good for you to get away for a bit."

I agreed, and soon my uncle, a pastor in California, arranged everything. I'd leave in a few weeks for the entire summer.

The idea of fishing and doing yard work at the resort appealed to me. Maybe I really could change. Another cousin of mine, Ben, had recently pulled out of the party scene, and he encouraged me to do the same. One night I even dreamed that Jesus saved me from my addiction.

But the pull of alcohol overpowered me. I made excuses and refused my uncle's help.

# Resound

"I'm worried about you, Jordan," my mom said to me one day after I returned home. "Someday you're going to have to answer for your choices." Her sobs wrenched my heart. "This life is not all there is, Jordan. Heaven is real. So is hell."

ॐॐॐ

I pushed aside my mom's concern and headed 30 miles down the road to the University of Iowa with my friend Adam to celebrate a buddy's birthday. It's been ranked by *TIME Magazine* as the number one party school in the nation. Like always, I drank with reckless abandon. Sometime in the early morning hours, Adam wanted to head home.

"Can I take your car, Jordan? I'll bring it back tomorrow."

"Nah." I scoffed at the idea. "Get in. I'll drive."

One of the girls from the party hopped in the backseat. "Can I get a ride home?"

I cranked up the bass and peeled out down the street. At the end of the block, I stopped at the stop sign, then blacked out. My foot pressed down on the accelerator, and we slammed into the concrete median.

"Dude, what are you doing?" Adam laughed.

I woke up with a jolt. My Chevy Monte Carlo pointed in the opposite direction.

I jumped out of the front seat. "What the heck?" I stared at the front tires, both flat. We weren't far from the party house, so I drove back on the rims, further damaging the tires.

The lights were out at the house when we returned. No one answered the door or the phone. Adam took off, leaving the two of us to sleep in the car.

Sunlight didn't help my hangover the next morning. I stumbled into the house, dreading the call to my father.

"Can you come get me?" I rehearsed my story. "I woke up to a couple flat tires."

"How'd that happen?" Skepticism laced my dad's words.

"Probably some kid out causing mischief," I lied.

"Really?" My dad didn't buy my answer.

"I don't know."

The Monte Carlo looked worse in the daylight. Dad drilled me all the way home, but I refused to crack.

The wreck unnerved me, but I couldn't admit my mounting fear that I was powerless to change. Guilt tore me up inside. *What if I'd killed someone?*

ఌఌఌ

I resolved to spend the following weekend sober, but dread filled me. How could I resist the offers to drink? On Thursday, buddies started calling me with weekend party plans.

When friends showed up with beer on Friday, I made excuses for not drinking. On Saturday, I holed up in my room, but sleep was impossible with all the noise. Sunday morning, I walked through a sea of drunken bodies.

"Where you going?" One of the guys woke up and saw me heading out the door.

"Church."

Another guy heard my answer, and their laughter followed me outside.

When my mom saw me enter the building, she ran up to me with open arms. Dad was out of town on business, so I followed her into the balcony of the sanctuary.

Something stirred deep within me as soon as the music started. My hands trembled during the pastor's message about God's love. The tremor moved throughout my body until I couldn't stop shaking.

"If anyone needs a fresh start, Jesus is waiting," the pastor finished with an invitation.

Unexpected tears sprung to my eyes and trickled down my face. I stood up. I'd never felt such a tangible presence of God before.

At the altar, a woman invited me to pray with her. I begged God to do something with my mess. I felt God's power wash over my own powerlessness, filling me with a strength not my own. God sent his son, Jesus, to take the punishment for all my mess-ups. I no longer had to fear death or hell. Jesus really was alive. And now I asked him to live in me.

❧❧❧

# Headlock

*Now what?*

I knew I needed to make changes, so I started with my living arrangement.

"I'm moving back with Mom and Dad," I told Jay a few weeks later, not sure how to explain the reason.

Jay was upset, but he only shrugged. We were more than brothers. We were best buds.

A few months earlier, I'd quit school to work full time as an electrical distributor, so work and moving kept me busy.

Then the weekend came, and a deep loneliness filled me. If God hadn't taken away my desire to party, alcohol would've won me back.

But God knew I needed a friend. Pastor Luke invited me to lunch after church the following Sunday. Sitting at the booth in Applebee's, the friendly New Zealander, who'd come with his wife to serve at our church, asked me my story. When I finished, he grinned from ear to ear.

"Mate, becoming a Christian is the best decision you could've made. God's got an amazing plan for you."

Pastor Luke's encouragement meant everything. Since I needed a place to connect, he invited me to help him with the youth ministry. The fit was perfect. Pastor Luke helped mentor me while I grew alongside the teens in Luke's small group. At an overnight retreat a few months later, I felt God nudging me to work in ministry full time. Finally, I knew what I wanted to do with my life.

I started an internship at the church and became Pastor Luke's right-hand man. After being around people whose only desire was to party, having friends who wanted to focus on God was a refreshing change. I never liked to speak in front of others, but Pastor Luke asked me to share my story at a youth service. Seeing kids respond was awesome. Soon, I was traveling to other youth groups with Pastor Luke and speaking. I was invited to speak in Mexico and India.

God's adventure for me was far more than I could have imagined.

๛๛๛

Two years later, Pastor Luke called me into his office after a Sunday service.

I wondered if I'd done something wrong.

"My wife and I are at a transition point in our lives. We sense God wanting us to plant a new church."

I leaned closer, listening as Pastor Luke shared more.

"Portland keeps coming to the front of our prayers." He looked me in the eye. "Alissa and I really love you, Jordan. We see the call of God on your life. If we move to Oregon, we need to start with a strong children's ministry for families."

My heart beat stronger in my chest. I'd never lived outside Iowa, but my experiences traveling to Mexico and India left me willing to go wherever God wanted to send me.

"Will you pray about joining us?"

"Yes." I didn't hesitate. "Yes, I'll come. And, yes, I'll

pray for confirmation that this is what God wants me to do."

In July of 2010, I packed my belongings in my Honda Accord and followed Pastor Luke and Alissa and two other families to Portland — a city I'd never even visited.

❧❧❧

Today — three years later — when I look around Resound, I marvel that God uses imperfect people like me, proof of God's goodness and grace. Broken people don't walk through our doors to pointing fingers of condemnation. They find a place that really resounds with God's love.

Surrendering to Jesus is the first step.

At Resound, we want to join people on the journey.

We all need teammates like Pastor Luke. Walking together, we are stronger.

Life — like wrestling — is a head game. Our opponent, who we identify as Satan, wants to cast doubt and condemnation. He wants to confuse us so we can't live lives that resound with the truth — that Jesus is our victory.

❧❧❧

"Come on. You can do it!" I bellowed, watching my wrestler get slammed on the mat. His opponent went for a headlock.

# Resound

Coaching wrestling at the high school level in Hillsboro, a city outside Portland, is enough to give me gray hair at 25.

I glanced at the clock. Thirty seconds. Sufficient time to score a victory. If only he could win the head game and pull out of the headlock.

*Come on. You can do it.*

My wrestler wriggled free and set up for my signature move — high crotch to a double leg take down.

*Bam.* His opponent lay pinned to the ground. The whistle blew.

"Yes!" I jumped up and down, screaming. "You won!"

Somewhere in a place I can't yet see, my ultimate Coach screams the same for me. *Yes! You won. Alcohol no longer has you in a headlock.*

The thought makes my heart pound in my chest. I can't quit grinning.

# The Greatest Addiction
## The Story of Daniel
### Written by Sharon Kirk Clifton

"Hey, Beth, I'm home. Wanna go to the state fair tonight?" No answer. "Got some friends with me from work. Beth?" Still no answer. Silence hung dense as a late September fog. Where could she be?

"Hey, guys, have a seat while I check upstairs. She must not have heard me." Then, louder, "Beth!"

All I heard in response was the pounding of my own heart.

Brandon, my boss, stood as I came down the stairs. "What's going on?"

"I don't know. She's —" Glancing off to my left, over the handrail, I saw a white envelope lying on top of the black entertainment center. A familiar pain gripped my gut. A few strides later, I had the envelope in my hands and was ripping it open.

*Daniel, I'm leaving, and I don't know if I'm coming back.* Then she'd scribbled an address where she'd left Joel, our young son.

"What?" I quickly ratcheted into panic overload. "That's clear on the other side of this complex. We don't even know those people. My baby's with strangers!"

Brandon came toward me, concern etching his face. "What's going on, Daniel?"

"I wish to God I knew." I shoved the note in his hand. "Listen, man, I gotta go get Joel. I'll be back."

"We'll wait here."

The next few minutes were a blur. I rushed to the address and pounded on the door. A woman I'd never seen before answered. Small children, including Joel, played on the floor behind her. "Oh, good, you're here," she said.

I dispensed with social amenities. "Did my wife tell you where she was going? What did she say?"

"No. She just said there was some kind of emergency and that you'd come pick up your son when you got home from work." Did the woman even know his name?

I swept him up in my arms and hurried back home. True to his word, Brandon, along with the other two co-workers who had anticipated a fun evening at the Oregon State Fair, were waiting for us.

"What happens now?" Brandon said.

"I've got to get Joel down to my parents' house in Salem. Before I even begin to deal with Beth, he's my number one priority."

Brandon patted my shoulder. "Sure. No problem. We'll take you."

I hurriedly packed a suitcase for Joel, and we headed for Salem. On the way down, I called my parents. Mom answered the phone. I told her what had happened.

"Oh, honey, I am so sorry," she said with a catch in her voice. "Have you contacted Beth's parents or anyone else in her family? Is she with them?"

"No. I don't know. You're the first I've called. I wanted you to know I'm on my way with Joel. He needs to stay with you while I figure all this out."

"Of course, dear. Oh, God bless you, Daniel."

*Yeah, right. God bless me.*

Why did she leave now? If she were going to take off, why not a month ago, when things were rocky for us? This past month had been better. I thought so, anyway.

After I'd collected several warm hugs from Mom and Dad and gotten Joel settled in, we went back to Portland. Brandon and the other two left after I assured them I'd be fine. Just fine. My wife was gone to … God knew where. My son was an hour away. I was alone in a townhouse that had suddenly become cavernous. But I'd be fine. Just fine.

I braced myself and called Beth's parents. Her mom answered. She sounded surprised at my news, but not as shocked as my own parents had been. Did I really hear an accusatory note in her mom's voice? No, she said, she hadn't heard from Beth and had no idea where she might be. What had I said to her? What had happened? What made her leave?

I wished Beth's sister, April, had a phone. The two were especially close, even though they were opposites — Beth being the quiet, reserved one and April, the wild child who had left home at 15, never to return, who had lived on the streets for a while, getting into her own set of troubles. I determined to go see April the next day, a Sunday.

When I told her what had happened, she freaked out,

questioning why her sister, the more predictable one, the sensible sibling, hadn't come to her, hadn't even hinted at what was going on inside her head, hadn't shared her plans to abandon her husband and son. She was frantic that Beth had been missing for more than 24 hours and no one had heard a word from her.

Okay. She wasn't at her parents' house or her sister's. There was one other place she would be.

With *that man*.

☙☙☙

This kind of thing wasn't supposed to happen. Not to someone like me. I'm a preacher's kid. God knows my parents did everything they could to assure a good outcome for their children. When the doors of the church were open, we were there. Hey, we were usually the ones who unlocked the doors.

They monitored any interaction with people or media that might tempt us to go astray. At times, they homeschooled us. At others, we attended a Christian school, depending on where we lived at the time. We moved around a lot.

They limited the time we could watch television. *Star Trek* and *Dr. Who* were parent-approved, but little else. Eventually, the television set was crammed to the back of a closet. Our only music was classical, instrumental jazz and Christian, but not even the latter if there was a whiff of rock about it.

# The Greatest Addiction

My brother Tyler and I were permitted to read very little fiction, so we plowed through a lot of non-fiction. People would ask how we came to know so much about the cultures of Greece, Rome and other ancient civilizations. When you live in Oregon, where it rains nine months out of the year, you're stuck inside most of the time. We were forced to use our brains, instead of vegging out in front of a TV. That was a good thing.

I graduated with honors from our local Christian high school at 16 and went straight to Chemeketa Community College. I followed that with a year at Salem Bible College, enrolled in pastoral studies — Dad's idea, not mine. My goal was to get my schooling done. My parents were bent on my getting locked into a church.

"Daniel, it doesn't have to be *our* church," Mom would often say. "Just find *a* church. Get connected."

After wandering from church to church for a while, I finally found one big enough that I could disappear into it. Mom often checked up on me on Sunday afternoons.

"Did you go to church?"

"Yeah, Mom. Of course I went to church." I said it even when it wasn't true. The Assembly of God was huge. Who could prove me wrong? With 3,000 members milling about, who'd know whether or not I was present on any given Sunday?

It was in the middle of a growth spurt. At first, I went to get my parents off my back, but I actually liked the place and the people. Many were making decisions to follow Jesus Christ. I got sucked in. *This is pretty cool,* I thought. Before I knew what was happening, I'd become a regular.

One day, a worship team leader came up to me.

"Daniel, you play any musical instruments?"

I told him I had played jazz trumpet growing up.

"Hmm. Well, we don't actually need a trumpet player right now, but …" He lifted a bass guitar from its stand and held it out to me. "Here, play this."

I put my hands up, palms out. "Oh, no, man. Sorry. I don't play bass guitar. I don't play guitar at all."

"Piece of cake, Daniel." He thrust the bass at me again. This time I took it. "I'll teach you all you need to know. Four chords. That's it, bro. You learn four chords and you're ready for most of the songs we do."

"Man, I don't know," I said, shaking my head.

Before I knew what was happening, I had learned those four basic chords and was playing with a team that went out to a nearby juvenile prison. It was great. That led to an invitation from the main worship leader to join the praise team for the church's youth.

Again, I tried to beg off. "I'm really not that good. I don't think I'm ready for that."

"You're just what we're looking for, Daniel. Someone who's not full of his own ego, someone who won't just perform or put on a show, someone who can really honor God with his music without calling attention to himself. It's not about you. It's about God."

As I tried to live in the way God would want me to, I knew I had to sever my relationship with a girl I had been seeing for a couple years. We were entirely too physical. I was trying to focus on God, and being with her, doing what we were doing, was getting in the way of that. Besides, lately I had been thinking about another girl, someone I had met at camp meeting on the teeter-totters long ago, when we were pre-teens. Beth. We were pen pals for several years, and our families often got together to hang out.

It was pretty obvious to anyone who paid attention that we liked each other. A lot. As time went by, though, life got in the way. The letters became less and less frequent until they ceased. Five or six years passed without my hearing from her.

Then my church scheduled a series of special meetings with a nationally-known preacher.

*Invite Beth,* something inside me prompted. I argued with myself, thinking it had been too long since we had corresponded. It hadn't ended badly. It had just ended. I knew nothing of her life. For all I knew, she was married, or at least involved with someone. *Invite Beth.*

I couldn't escape the nudging, so I called the only number I had for her, her parents' home phone. After all those years, I still remembered it. My fingers punched in the digits with no hesitancy.

Her mom answered. Beth was at work. She said she'd tell her daughter I'd called.

Later that evening, the phone rang.

"Hi, Daniel. It's me, Beth."

Ah, it had been so long since I'd heard that soft, quiet

voice. I hoped she couldn't hear my heart pounding like a frenetic timpani, but how could she not?

After the usual polite chitchat, I invited her to the special meetings at church.

"Sure, I'll come," she said. "Sounds like fun."

She came for the Sunday evening service, and from then on, we spent a lot of time together. Our friendship picked up where it had left off years before. The trip from friendship to love was a short one.

By October 1998, I knew she was the one for me, so I asked her dad for permission to court her. He said yes, so one cold, rainy night at the end of the month, after I had locked up the church and we were walking toward my car, I went down on one knee, took her hand in mine and asked her to marry me.

Her tears mingled with the raindrops. "Yes! Yes! Yes, Daniel, I'll marry you." I rose and drew her close. Had it stopped raining by then? I don't recall. The scent of her hair mingled with the ozone smell of the mist as I wrapped my arms around her and we kissed.

Then I held her at arms' length. "Hey, wanna do something only slightly crazy?"

She laughed. "Sure. Why not? Whatcha got in mind?"

"Let's go to the campground where we first met. It's only about 10 miles away. Want to?"

"I do!" We were like two kids, off on a secret adventure.

Within 15 minutes, we stood at the teeter-totters where I'd first spoken to that shy 10-year-old girl. The same qualities that had captivated me then still did: namely, her quiet grace — so unlike the other boisterous girls her age — her gentle demeanor and her serious reserve. We talked long into the night and rode the teeter-totter.

In April 1999, I married the girl of my dreams. "Therefore, what God has joined together, let no man put asunder." I think that's how it goes. Or is supposed to, anyway.

ॐॐॐ

Life was good in those early months. We moved to Salem, where I worked as a lab technician for an optical company. I loved the job. Nonetheless, when a friend of mine accepted an offer to be senior pastor at a small church in Astoria and invited us to come along to help out, we accepted. Beth and I worked with the teens, and I also did some percussion with the worship team. Whatever I could do to benefit my friend and the church, I did.

Money was tight, so I got a job at Burger King. I also welded for a man who designed and made some pretty cool jewelry in the shape of a cross.

We still struggled financially. Beth got a job at Dairy Queen, though she was pregnant. We joked that we had the fast-food market covered. But it wasn't enough. Eventually, I took on two full-time jobs — one as a server at Denny's, and another as a care provider at a retirement home. Neither job paid very well, and with a baby coming, we didn't know what we were going to do.

Work. Eat. Sleep. Work. Eat. Sleep. No longer could I help my friend at church. Joel was born while we were in Astoria, but I was working so much, I had little time to spend with him and Beth and none for church. Or God.

Joel wasn't a month old before the phone call came that changed our lives. I accepted an offer to work at Intel in Hillsboro. This job meant more money than I'd ever made. It also required another move, but it was worth it.

My mother's calls continued once we moved to the Portland area.

"So, have you found a church home yet?" she'd ask.

"Not yet, Mom," I'd say. "It takes time. We're looking."

"Are you really?"

"Yes, really."

Sort of. It was a priority to her, but not to us. Oh, we visited around, even going to the church Beth had grown up in, but we knew — I knew, anyway — it wasn't a good fit for us. We intended to find a church home eventually, for Joel's sake, if not our own. The calls kept coming. Did Mom have a list of questions written down that she kept by the phone? It seemed so, because she called most Sundays and reviewed the litany.

"Did you go to church today?"

"What did the preacher speak on?"

"What songs did you sing?"

I was glad she couldn't see me roll my eyes, as I bluffed

my way through her interrogation on the Sundays when we stayed home.

I loved my job at Intel and looked forward to a bright future with the company. I made enough that we could enjoy some of the shiny stuff. Unfortunately, it distracted us from some really important issues.

Then, everything went crazy. Intel suffered an economic downturn. The market for PCs and laptops took a huge dive. The corporation laid off 4,000 employees in just under a year. I hadn't been there long. "Last hired, first fired" kicked in, and I was out. Since I'd made good money while the party lasted, my unemployment checks amounted to a tidy sum and kept us afloat for a while. We drifted on that cushion for about a year. Jobs were hard to come by.

During that time, Beth and I participated in massive multiplayer online role-playing games (MMORPGs). We each had our own computer, so we could play cooperatively. If she stopped engaging in the action, I knew it. One day, I noticed she wasn't playing.

"Hey, Beth, what are you doing? The game's going on without you."

"Huh? Oh. I'm … uh … in the chat room."

"Oh. Okay. That's cool. I just wondered."

I didn't think too much about it. I'd been in the chat room a few times, too, though I was more interested in playing the game than chatting with the other players. Beth's visits, however, became more frequent and longer — so much so that the game was secondary to the chat. If I got up to get something, she'd guard her screen or X out of the chat window.

"Who are you talking to?"

"Just a friend, Daniel. Is that okay with you?"

From her defensive tone, I was fairly certain the *friend* was a man, but I didn't want to jump to conclusions.

Just about the time the unemployment from Intel ran out, I got a job with National Vision. Once again, I would earn good money doing optics, something I loved to do. It meant another move, this time to Vancouver, Washington.

One day, I came home to find Beth talking on the phone to someone. From the look on her face when I walked in, I knew I had intruded on a private conversation. She spoke softly into the mouthpiece as she walked to another room. I followed her.

"Who're you talking to?" Ouch. Even I could hear the edge in my voice.

She ignored my question, speaking to the person on the phone, instead. "I have to go. Now." She disconnected.

"Who. Was. That?"

"A friend."

"A *friend*? Which friend?"

"You're being very rude. Do you know that?"

"Answer me."

She pivoted to walk away. "Not when you use that tone of voice. You need to calm down."

"D*** it, Beth! Just tell me who you were talking to. Was it your chat room friend?"

She whirled to face me. "So what if it was?"

"Does he know you're married? With a baby, for crying out loud?"

"Daniel, I really don't want to discuss this with you."

"I don't doubt that." I turned up the decibels. "Does he know you're married?"

"You're scaring me."

"Just answer the question."

"Yes! Yes, he knows!"

"Who called who?"

"He did."

"How did he know our number?"

"I gave it to him."

"You did *what*? You gave him our home phone number? Beth, what were you thinking? Stupid! That was just stupid! What's his name? Where does he live?"

She scowled, then pressed her mouth into a hard line. Where was my beautiful Beth?

I turned away. I tried to ignore the gut pain that had plagued me most of my life, especially in stressful times. I wanted to rage against this whole situation, to rail at God. *Help me! I cannot handle this!* I wanted to pummel the face of that man, whoever he was.

When I again turned toward her, her cheeks were wet.

"Beth, please, please don't do this." My voice was softer, more controlled than I felt. "Please. For God's sake. For our sake."

The next time I walked in on a phone conversation, I yanked the phone from Beth's hand and shot a string of invectives into his ear, telling him exactly what I thought of him. "Do not call *my* wife again." I screamed it. Surely the neighbors heard, but I didn't care.

The next month was uneventful, to the point that I allowed myself to be lulled into thinking I had fixed it. Now things were getting better. Beth and I were healing, I told myself.

Right up to the day she split.

ॐॐॐ

After my visit with April, ascertaining that Beth wasn't with her and she didn't know any more about her sister's disappearance than I did, I immediately called the Washington State Police, not knowing if they could or would do anything to help. Would they blow me off and say, "Sir, she is an adult. She's free to come and go at will?" Those fears were allayed when they listened carefully as I gave them my story, telling about the MMORPGs, the chat room conversations, the phone calls — and my reaction to them. They took down information about her family, too.

"What's the name of the man whom you believe your wife is with?" the officer said.

"I don't know."

"Where does he live?"

"I'm sorry, but I don't know that, either. It may be a good thing I don't. I think it's a Southern state. Mississippi, maybe. Or Missouri. I'm sorry. I really don't know."

# The Greatest Addiction

"That's okay. You say he called?"

"Yes, sir."

"Your home phone or a cell phone?"

"Home phone. Ground line."

"Sir, we cannot do much until your wife has been missing three days. Rest assured, we will do everything in our power to find out what's going on and get her back home."

How would I ever make it through the next few days? That first evening, I went over to my brother Tyler's place, which turned out to be a bad idea. He had a party going on. I got wasted. The vodka flowed like water, and I was thirsty. And I was the brother who didn't drink. Not normally, anyway. But then, *normal* walked out the door with Beth. Somehow, I made it back to our apartment.

My mind kept going to the darkest places. This man, this monster, who was he? He could have been a 60-something letch or a 20-something punk, a serial killer or a convicted rapist. What if he had lured her away from all she knew, ravaged her and imprisoned her in a dank cellar or an abandoned warehouse somewhere? What if she were dead, her body lying in a shallow grave hidden by a thicket? *No! Stop thinking like that.* Don't people know when a missing loved one is dead or alive? Don't they have some kind of mystical internal confirmation one way or the other? But it was so out of character for Beth not to call her parents to let them know she was okay. What was I saying? This whole mess was out of character.

On day three, I was on my way to Salem to pick up

Joel when my cell phone rang. It was Beth. I had to pull the car off the road because I was too overwhelmed to drive and talk to her at the same time. *Lord, help me,* I prayed.

"Beth, why? Why did you leave?"

"Because I was mad at you."

"When are you coming back?"

"I'm not sure. I'm not sure that I am."

"Have you called your parents?"

"No. Not yet."

"You've got to. Right away. You have no idea what kind of hell this has put people through. Your parents, April, your family, they're freaking out. We didn't even know if you were dead or alive, Beth. Do you get that? You split without telling anyone where you were going. You left your son with a stranger. No one has heard from you. Do you have a clue what everyone is going through?"

"Yeah. I guess."

Then I asked how she had gotten there. He had sent her a one-way airline ticket.

"Oh." Dead air. "Beth?"

"Yeah."

"Do you still love me at all?"

"No."

More dead air.

"Call your mom."

We disconnected, and I phoned my parents. Mom answered. I told her about Beth's call and asked if she could keep Joel another week. He didn't need to be around a daddy who felt as I did right then, and I needed time to sort things out. Turning the car around, I headed back to Vancouver.

At the townhouse, the ghosts of happier days haunted every room. I couldn't sleep in our bed. It was too depressing because she wasn't there. It was too big, too empty. I might get lost in the sheets. The first couple of nights, I just sat in the closet and stared at the ceiling. In the bathroom, the scent of strawberries still lingered from her shampoo and body wash. I could smell her hairspray, too.

My thoughts turned to suicide. I had a dull knife, and I kept hitting my hand with it, thinking. When people called to check on me, I let the phone go to the machine. I shut everyone out, including my parents and my life-long best friend, Brandon. I stopped eating. I had lost my way. Any crumbs I'd dropped along the trail had been devoured by crows. Beth was gone, and not one crumb of her love remained.

I decided suicide was not an option because of Joel. That little guy was down to one parent, and I was it. I would never leave or forsake him. Someone else said that once. Who was it? Oh, yeah. Jesus.

I forced myself to go to work. Somewhere along the line, I had learned no matter how crazy your life becomes, you keep your personal stuff separate from your professional life. You act responsibly. You do your job. Then you can go home with a clear conscience, curl into a fetal position and cry yourself to sleep, if need be.

Sometime during that week I started calling out to God again. I talked to him, but I also listened. I got my Bible down, dusted the cobwebs off and began reading it. It was time I considered an ugly reality. Divorce. What did the Bible say about it?

The index in the back pointed me to the Gospel of Matthew. Licking my index finger, I flipped through the thin pages to chapter 19 and read the first 10 verses. Verse 9 permits divorce in the case of sexual immorality, but I couldn't get over verse 8: "Jesus replied, 'Moses permitted you to divorce your wives because your hearts were hard. But it was not this way from the beginning.'" *Permitted you,* he said. I could almost hear a parent's exasperated sigh in those two words. Even in cases of adultery, divorce was not God's preferred solution.

I wouldn't give up on Beth or our marriage. I would fight to reclaim her heart. Court her again, if need be. Woo her. The battle would begin with me on my knees, praying.

&#10052;&#10052;&#10052;

Beth came back, but not to me. She stayed with her parents. Even as I prayed and read my Bible, depression clung like a cloak I couldn't shrug from my shoulders, try as I might. I didn't want to eat. Nothing tasted good. If I did eat, I vomited it back up. I lost 40 pounds in a month, and the agony I felt in my lower gut increased in frequency, as well as intensity.

# The Greatest Addiction

Joel stayed with my parents in Salem, so I joined him there, commuting to my job. I could no longer stand to be in our apartment, anyway.

Beth had been back about three weeks when I decided to go see her. We'd talked on the phone a couple times by then, but I wanted to see her in person. Not knowing how the conversation would go, I determined I would be Christ-like, no matter what, to let God lead the conversation as much as possible. Surprisingly, we had a good heart-to-heart.

"Beth, I have to ask, why did you come back?"

"Dad," she said. "He called me and said he was sending me a plane ticket. You know Dad. He said" — here she deepened her voice slightly — 'If you don't use that ticket, I'm driving down there and bringing you back myself.'" She smiled.

"I'm glad you're at least back in the area."

The smile disappeared.

"Are you staying?"

She shrugged.

I dreaded the answer to my next question. "Are you still in contact with ... what's his name?"

She nodded. "Daniel, you're ... so thin." Was she trying to change the subject?

"Yeah. Well, food hasn't exactly been a priority lately." Some emotion flickered across her face, but vanished before I could interpret it.

"How much have you lost?"

"Forty pounds."

"Daniel! That's too much. Have you seen a doctor? You have a good job now."

"No insurance, yet, though, so, no, I haven't seen a doctor."

"Oh." I hoped that was concern I saw and not pity. *Please, Lord, don't let it be pity.*

"Beth, what about us?"

"I'm not sure there is an *us*. I don't know if I want there to be an *us*. But I have to tell you something."

"Yeah?"

"Yeah. Oh, man, how do I say this?"

"Just say it."

She sighed deeply and rubbed her lips together. "As soon as I stepped on the plane to leave, I knew it was a mistake."

"What?" I felt as though someone had thrown a medicine ball at my stomach. "Then why didn't you just turn around and walk off? Beth!"

She stood up and walked across the room, wrapping her arms around herself. "Because I'd already committed to leaving."

I stood now, too, and rolled my eyes toward heaven. "Oh, God, this is crazy."

"I know. I know. But I didn't think you'd take me back. You certainly won't ever forgive me or want me once I tell you that … he and I, well … we were intimate."

I wanted to whirl her around, pull her into my arms and show her exactly how fast I'd take her back. But I didn't.

Instead, I said something about how forgiving Christ is toward us when we're unfaithful to him. Then we said our cordial but stilted goodbyes, and I left.

❧❧❧

My health continued to decline. Finally, I acquiesced to pressure from my parents, who didn't buy my self-diagnosis of bronchitis or the flu. To get them off my back — and because they offered to pay for the visit — I went to see their doctor, who immediately sent me over to the hospital for some tests. He said I was in pretty bad shape. When the test results came back, the doctor then ordered an ultrasound. At some point, my appendix had exploded, I had two gall stones, a hernia and Crohn's disease. The Crohn's had plagued me since birth, according to the doctor, though it had never been diagnosed before. It was the cause of the severe lower intestinal pain I suffered so often.

I was admitted to the hospital, and my parents called Beth to let her know what was going on. They prepped me for surgery, and while I was waiting to be rolled in, Beth arrived. Her eyes were red-rimmed, as though she'd been crying. She walked slowly over to my bedside.

"Oh, Daniel, I'm so very, very sorry." She spoke barely above a whisper. "For everything."

"It's okay." I reached for her hand. "It's okay."

She stayed with me for the hour prior to my surgery. Neither one of us said much. We didn't need to. After all, we were husband and wife. Sometimes words don't have to be spoken. Sometimes they just get in the way.

When I returned and awakened, she was still there. I knew she would be. My beautiful Beth was back to stay. We moved home and began seeing a wonderful marriage counselor, who also was a follower of Christ.

Lily, our second child, was born in 2003. Mom said she was the very image of me as an infant. That made me extremely happy, considering all that had happened over the past year. Her birth went a long way toward healing our marriage.

We regularly attended a church in Portland. Once again, those four basic guitar chords came in handy because I played with the worship team. The pastor taught a Bible study on the Song of Solomon, an especially timely pursuit for us at that time.

Celia, our third child, came along in 2006, which was a financially challenging year for us. I had changed jobs. Now I worked for a manufactured home company. It started out well enough, with my selling a home my first month with the company, earning me a healthy commission. If I could have done that every month, we would have been fine, but the manufactured home market in the area took a nosedive following some financing scandals that had occurred in the area, so things were getting tough. The job wasn't paying the bills.

My Crohn's cycled, sometimes causing severe problems, but then easing up after awhile. Stress definitely exacerbated it, and I was stressed over the job situation, so

# The Greatest Addiction

I was in excruciating pain and having internal bleeding three to five times a week. It was like having up to 24 ulcers throughout the lower intestines. Bad diet and certain foods caused flare-ups, too.

On Thanksgiving 2006, I was hurting badly when I went over to see my brother. He was smoking some weed. He could tell I was in a lot of pain.

"Want to try some of this?" he said.

"Oh, man, I don't know."

"Hey, it might help the hurt. Give it a try." Medical cannabis was legal in Oregon by that time.

I tried it, and it did help. "I can't feel my stomach." That was the first time I had used, and it would be a year before I did it again.

I made four devastating choices in 2007.

First, since the manufactured home job didn't pan out, I went to culinary school. Why not? I loved cooking, and it seemed to me that the people who succeeded in life had studied to learn a trade. I had no idea what I was getting into. People with families shouldn't be chefs. I spent very little time at home with Beth and the kids. I had to get a part-time job, too, so my life was consumed with school and work. Sometimes I got only two or three hours' sleep a night.

Second, I eased away from church because I worked Sundays. I didn't suddenly make a conscious decision to stop going to church. I wasn't mad at God. I believed in him. I wasn't walking away from my faith. I just didn't think I had time. I had scheduled my life so that I didn't have time. How could I let something like this happen? I'd heard the Bible all my life. I knew how to look, sound, walk, talk and smell like a Christian. So what was wrong with me? I knew the rules. Why did I have so much trouble following them?

Third, I started smoking pot. Not just once in awhile, either, but all the time. Oh, but I was doing it for medical reasons. It eased the pain of the Crohn's. And maybe, if I smoked more, I would never have to deal with the hurt in my gut. As time went by, I knew I wasn't doing it only to dull the pain. It was fun. And I was addicted.

Fourth, I rented a room from April and her husband, so I'd have a place to crash. It was closer to school and work. The problem was twofold. I was living away from home, and I wasn't living a life that honored Christ. I developed an addiction to online pornography. Of all the problems I struggled with, porn was the worst. Even as I did it, I loathed it. Porn enslaves its addicts. *I don't want to do this,* I said to myself as I clicked all the right links. *I do not want to do this.*

Having finished culinary school, I gave up the room and moved back home. One day, I called Beth aside to talk with her.

"I have to tell you something," I said.

"Okay."

"I smoke pot."

"Why?"

"It really helps with my Crohn's. Hon, it's amazing."

She nodded. I could tell she didn't like the idea, but

she was reluctant to say much, perhaps because of her history.

She already knew about the pornography, because I had mentioned it before, but she didn't know the frequency of it or the depth of its bondage.

I started playing trumpet with a hip-hop band, and we all smoked weed and partied. We had some crazy times. So I moved up the pot ladder — from hit to bowl to "honey," a very potent form. Sometimes I'd do a couple bowls and drive home. I don't know how I kept from hurting someone because I was really stoned. I did mushrooms, too.

In 2009, our fourth child, Eden, was born. At that point, everything I did revolved around marijuana. I scheduled my days around my habit. Some people need their cup of Joe first thing in the morning. I needed a hit. I'd say to my family, "Hey, let's go to the zoo," all the while figuring the best place to smoke a joint there. I was obsessed with it. Of course, the porn addiction kept its iron grip on my soul, too.

My parents were in the dark about both the drugs and the porn. Sure, they knew I wasn't in church, but they accepted my excuse that I was working all the time.

Sometime in 2011, we decided to do the church thing again. It would be good for the kids to have the "church experience." We visited several churches around the Portland area, including Resound. The people met together in a theater. It was all good — the preaching, the music, the casual atmosphere and the people, too. My routine became go to church, come home and go to the bathroom to get high. I never smoked before church.

God was drawing me to him and to the Bible. Often, I'd read the Bible while smoking pot in the car before going into work. Then, I'd go to my car at lunchtime, eat and read God's written words to us while taking a hit.

Mom and Dad made sure we had plenty of Christian books on hand. I'd say thanks and toss each new volume onto a shelf. A couple weeks would go by, and one of them, usually Mom, would say, "Did you read that book I gave you?"

"Aw, you know what, Mom?" I'd say. "I haven't gotten around to it yet. I've been so busy, you know. No time." She'd just purse her lips and shake her head.

One book she'd given us was called *Resound Portland: Seven Stories, One Sound.* One Sunday in July 2012, we decided to visit Resound again. The pastor mentioned some of the stories from the book during his message, and I thought they sounded pretty interesting.

*We have the book,* I thought. *Thank you, Mom.*

For years, she had plagued me with her list of Sunday afternoon questions. I considered the reminders to read the books she had given us as just another way of nagging. But not today. As soon as we got home, instead of smoking a joint, I went looking for the book. There it was. I blew the dust from its cover and cracked it open. By afternoon's end, I had read the whole book. The stories were amazing. They were all the more meaningful because they were true. The people were real.

# The Greatest Addiction

*Wow,* I thought, as I closed it. *I can't believe these people went through such horrible things and came out at the other end victorious. Some of these people were probably with me in the service this morning. That is so awesome! Any one of these stories could be a movie. I'd watch it. I'd buy it!* Three of the testimonies especially connected with me and touched me to my core: "Running Shoes," "Awakening" and "647." An overwhelming feeling of peace — the kind of peace only God can give — washed over me after I finished the book.

I looked over at my wife. "Beth, I can never smoke pot again. Never."

"Good." She grinned at me. "Why not?"

"Because it draws my attention away from Jesus Christ."

Ironically, before church that morning, I had decided to take a breather from smoking. I'd finished my last bag of weed. That day, I dumped all my paraphernalia. Everything connected with the habit went in the trash.

I had a God-sent epiphany. I had been doing it all wrong. Finally, I realized I'm not perfect, and I'm not going to be perfect in this life. When I try to make myself perfect, I'm negating what Jesus Christ did on the cross. He paid for those sins, those things that break God's law and heart, because he knew we were going to do them. When we're legalistic, we're saying, "I'm going to carry this burden myself."

Jesus says, "No. That's why I came. That's why I died on the cross. I already paid for *all* those wrong things you've done." Of all the years I spent in church, being raised in it and serving on worship teams, the message of grace, God's unmerited favor poured out on us, was never revealed, or at least I never picked up on it. I was so focused on forcing myself not to sin, instead of centering my attention on Christ.

To do this, I needed a plan in place. I knew the desire for a hit would come. If nothing else, the pain of Crohn's would tempt me back to it. I asked the Lord how to deal with that. The answer was clear: with the Bible, the written word of God. I kept my Kindle in the bathroom. It has the Bible loaded on it. When I felt the need for weed, I went in to read. I still do.

Since I handed the reins of my life over to Christ that Sunday in 2012, everything is different. A great burden lifted from my shoulders. He blesses every aspect of my life. He has helped me financially. I'm working at a job I love, making more than I've ever made. My family life is sweet. Our awesome God even healed me of Crohn's.

Beth and I finally have the kind of marriage we talked about that rainy night by the teeter-totters. I love my lady, and she loves me! God is equipping me for my role as faithful leader of our home. We're both growing in faith and learning to live a life that honors Christ.

One evening I sprang something major on Beth.

"Hon, what would you say to our leading a small group Bible study?"

"What? Here? Us?"

"Sure. Why not us? We love small groups, and you

know that the person who leads a Bible study learns the most from that study. Want to?"

She thought about it a minute, then flashed me a broad smile. "Sure, why not!" Now she's as excited about that prospect as I am.

And something else happened. About six months after I turned the management of my life over to Jesus Christ, I sat down at my computer to play a game. That's when it hit me.

*I don't want to go to a porn site. I have absolutely no desire for that. None! And haven't for six months!* God had severed the chains that kept me bound and purged away the self-loathing that accompanies that insidious addiction. To God be the glory. Great things he has done!

I do have a new addiction, however. The greatest addiction. Reading and studying the written words of God.

# The Drive for Freedom
## The Story of Carlos
### Written by Joy Steiner Moore

"Stay here," the man whispered, holding a finger to his lips. "Do not make any noise."

He looked each one of us in the eyes, and I understood the unspoken words that were clearly behind his gaze: *Trust me.*

His car keys jingled lightly in his hand as he reached up to close the trunk, and I watched wide-eyed with fear as the door came down upon us and latched, trapping us in the darkness.

The teenage girl next to me whimpered, and someone reacted with a sharp "Shhh." There were seven of us squeezed into the trunk, and I had no idea how the man had gotten us to fit. It was like a human puzzle that he had masterfully and artfully pieced together.

The car started, and we felt the rumble of the road beneath us. I don't know how fast the car was going, but in my mind, it wasn't fast enough.

We could barely breathe in the smothering heat. The smell of body odor was almost overwhelming. Sweat poured off my face, and a small bead of perspiration trickled down my neck, causing it to itch. But because my arms were trapped, I couldn't reach up to scratch it. After a few minutes, I realized I could no longer feel my legs; my feet were pinned at an odd angle under someone's body. I

151

tried to wiggle my toes, but I couldn't tell if they were moving or not.

The miserable minutes dragged on, eventually turning into hours. I had lost all track of time. Our bodies were damp and hot, and our sweat mingled. As hard as we were pressed together, we seemed to be melting into one another. We felt every single bump in the road, rising and falling and leaning as one unit. The air seemed less breathable with every second that passed. But above all, the hardest part was staying silent. We couldn't even utter a moan.

*What if I don't live through this?*

It was a strange thought. Until now, it had only been my discomfort at stake and, if we got caught, deportation back to Mexico. But now I was starting to understand that we could suffocate here. I was risking my life, and death was a real possibility. And 14 was too young to die.

Was it worth all this? For freedom? I didn't know. I squeezed my eyes shut, determined to keep living, keep breathing, keep surviving.

*When will this nightmare end?*

"Carlos, you caught one!"

"Yes!" I beamed, holding up my fishing line to show off the small trout I had just reeled in. My older brother patted me on the back to show his approval, while my dad and uncles called out their congratulations from where they fished farther down the river. It wasn't a large catch, but it would definitely add to the dinner bucket.

We lived in a small village in Oaxaca, Mexico, an eight-hour drive from Mexico City. I was the sixth of 12 children, so of course, money was scarce. Even at my young age of 7, I worked in the agave fields at the local tequila ranch with my uncles to help bring in extra money for my family.

But today was Sunday, our day off, so it was our time to hunt and fish. We also drank lots and lots of tequila — not just on Sundays, but every day. It helped drown the pain and exhaustion from working hard and living poor in the hot Mexican jungle.

In the evening, my mom cooked our fish over the fire. The feast tasted delicious to me, even more than normal since I had contributed. As the women cleaned up after the meal, one of my uncles poured some hard liquor in my glass. He winked at me and then leaned lazily back against the stone wall of our tiny three-room house. I took a sip and, like the many times before, relished the tangy burn of the alcohol as it slid down my throat, looking forward to the buzz that was to come.

❧❧❧

When I was 9, my dad paid a lot of money for my sister and me to go away to school. From our remote village, we had to walk for two days, then hitchhike three hours by car. I was okay there for a while, but when the school officials caught me drinking, they kicked me out. My sister didn't want to stay there alone, so she came home, too.

My dad had always had a temper and had never been afraid to beat any of us. But the whipping that awaited me when I got home was unlike any other. I decided to run away and live with my sister and brother-in-law in a different village.

I worked on another tequila ranch, cutting firewood and doing other farm work. I made my own money, which I quickly spent on alcohol. I liked to experiment with different kinds, and it didn't take long for me to learn that I liked them all. They made me feel good. Sometimes when I was short on money, I would mix the drinks with Coca-Cola. Other times, my brother-in-law would buy drinks for me. Even though the hangovers were horrible, I couldn't seem to stop. It was addicting.

A man from a neighboring town came to take a vacation in our village when I was 14. Of course, any outsider was fascinating, and we soon became friends. When it was time for him to return home, he had an extra plane ticket, and he asked me to join him.

There was nothing keeping me in my village, and the thrill of my first airplane ride, not to mention the adventure of going to the United States, made it an easy yes for me. Besides, there were a couple of other boys I knew who were going.

We flew to Tijuana and crossed the border on foot while the border patrol officers were switching shifts at 11 p.m. Easy enough. But they said that the hardest part was still ahead.

We were dropped off at a house in San Diego and told to wait for our driver for the next leg of the journey. Immigration officials regularly patrolled the highways between San Diego and Los Angeles, operating checkpoints. The guards at those checkpoints were not nearly as forgiving as the overworked officers at the border. If we got pulled over and caught without immigration paperwork, they would send us back to Mexico on the spot.

Our driver arrived at 3 a.m. He backed his car into the driveway and then walked around the back to open up the trunk. He was very businesslike. For him, this was an everyday transaction.

"You are going to go in the trunk." He motioned to all of us.

I could feel my eyes widen, and I exchanged nervous glances with the others — five other teenagers and one grown woman. But there wasn't time or reason to argue. This was the price we were paying for our freedom.

"You first," the man ordered, choosing one of my friends. The boy climbed in and squeezed himself against the interior wall of the trunk. One by one, we all followed, piling in as we were directed, as tightly as we could, until we were packed in like sardines. Silently I wondered how long this trip to Los Angeles would take.

We endured the smothering, hot misery of the trunk for what seemed like an eternity. We were soaked in our own sweat and that of everyone around us. Just as I was beginning to believe I might suffocate to death, the car slowed down. It seemed like we were no longer on the highway. The car turned right, and then left, and then right again. The turns were making me feel sick to my stomach.

*I don't think I can make it anymore.*

We came to a stop. Inwardly I cheered, thinking, *Just a few more minutes. Surely just a few more minutes.*

It was longer than a few minutes, and still, I survived. I just kept breathing. I suffered through.

When the driver finally opened the trunk, a full five hours had passed. Cool air descended upon us, and we breathed deeply, almost lapping it up like thirsty puppies. The intensity of the oxygen made me lightheaded.

One at a time, the driver helped us out of the trunk and into the dingy garage of the house in LA where he had taken us.

My legs felt like rubber. I could barely stand on them, and it would take the rest of the day for the kinks to work themselves out so I could walk again.

But we were here, we were alive and we were free.

ॐॐॐ

For two years, I lived in Los Angeles with the man who had given me the plane ticket. I couldn't speak English, and job opportunities were limited for a Spanish-speaking teenager. So I did a variety of things, including construction and working in clothing factories. I made about $15 per day.

I worked with a couple who often invited me to go to church with them.

"Jesus loves you and wants to change your life," they said.

But I hadn't had good experiences with churchgoers. My own parents were Catholic, and my aunts and uncles back home were Seventh Day Adventist. But that hadn't changed the fact that the men in my family always beat the women. I didn't want anything to do with that.

Instead, I drank a lot and started hanging out with gang members. I was beginning to feel like my life was going nowhere, but I didn't know how to change that. So I kept drowning those feelings in more alcohol.

❧ ❧ ❧

"If you come with me to Colorado Springs, we can make more money than we're making right now," one of my co-workers said one day.

"Doing what?" I asked.

"Construction. Stucco."

"You're sure it's more money?"

"Yes, it is. Good money."

So I said goodbye to my generous friend who had given me a good home in California, and at the age of 17, I traveled to Colorado Springs, where I was promised that "the grass was greener." We lived with the boss, and he gave us food to eat and a place to sleep. We worked hard — Monday through Saturday, from 6 a.m. to 6 p.m. But the money wasn't better. In fact, there seemed to be no money. Other than our food and board, the boss only paid us every six months or so, and it was much less money than he had promised my friend and me. I began to sink deeper into depression.

*Is this how life will always be for me? Will I always be stuck, living at the mercy of dishonest Americans?*

Worst of all, because of the language barrier, I didn't know how to do anything about the situation. I didn't have the courage to confront my boss, and since I was an illegal immigrant, I knew I didn't have any legal rights. So when I got frustrated, I'd go drink. And once I started, I couldn't stop. It was nothing for me to drink 30 beers in one sitting. I'd smoke pot, too — whatever it took to escape my hopeless reality.

But when I learned that the boss was putting our money in CDs and gaining interest for himself, that was the final straw. I had worked for him for two years by this point, and I was done. I confronted him, but it did not go well. I was too angry to speak calmly and rationally, and I lost my temper. He paid me eventually, but he wasn't happy about it, and I was out of a job. It was time to move on.

I was basically homeless, floating from place to place, wherever I heard there was work and good pay for someone like me. My goal was to make it to North Carolina, but I ended up stuck in Illinois, living in a

# The Drive for Freedom

Greyhound bus station for about a month.

One evening, I wandered through downtown Chicago looking for a liquor store, when I came across three other young Hispanic guys who were new to the area. We started talking, and they told me that they were driving back from Canada. After exchanging stories, they asked me if I wanted to come along with them to Oregon. Since I was alone and living in a bus station, Oregon sounded good to me.

࿐࿐࿐

The next few years in Portland were rough. My new friends and I drank heavily. We went to bars and strip clubs all the time. I got jobs as a painter and anything else that didn't require me to know or speak English. It was basically more of the same. I was stuck in an endless cycle of working and drinking and being very unhappy.

When I was 22, I got sick and ended up in the hospital for 15 days. But while I was there, none of my friends came to visit me. I felt very alone.

*Why are they not coming?*

It seemed that the guys only wanted to hang around when I bought liquor for them. Since I couldn't buy alcohol from my hospital bed, there was no reason for them to visit. After a while, I came to the sad realization that they weren't really my friends after all.

The days ticked by, and through my hospital window, I watched the world go on without me. Nobody even seemed to notice my absence. For 15 days, as my body continued to fight my illness, I stared glumly at the ceiling and thought about how sad my life actually was.

సౌసౌసౌ

A few months later, my depression grew even deeper. Overall, I was angry with how my life was turning out. Being illegal, it felt like I was always on the run. Since I didn't speak English, I felt constantly confused. I hadn't had a real home since I was 9 years old. And now I didn't have any friends. I blamed my dad for making me want to leave home in the first place, and I was ashamed of my alcohol addiction and how tied to it I was.

So after a heavy night of drinking, I found myself on the Fremont Bridge, half hung over, ready to end my life. My right foot slammed onto the gas pedal, and the car picked up speed. I passed beneath the big arch, the bridge's suspension cords flying past me.

*Faster. Faster.*

There was a nasty presence behind me, urging me on.

*That's right. Now drive off the bridge.*

It would take only a flick of my wrist to cross the other lanes of traffic, crash through the side rail at high speed and sail off the bridge into the water below.

I felt sick to my stomach. An icy chill passed through my body. I could feel my heart pounding in my chest as my breaths started to come more rapidly. I couldn't think straight.

# The Drive for Freedom

*Come on. Do it,* the presence urged. The air in the car seemed heavy and dark. Evil.

Suddenly, I gave in, my hands turning the steering wheel slightly to the left so that the car headed for the far wall of the bridge.

But in that instant, very quietly, deep in my heart, was another voice speaking as well. A very different voice.

"Hey, wait!" it said gently. "You still have hope!"

I slammed on the brakes. The car came to a stop in the far left lane, just a few feet from the railing. My body shook, suddenly free of the despair which had almost guided me to my death.

*I still have hope? What hope?*

All I knew was that I was physically and mentally drained. Overcome with exhaustion and a pounding headache from my hangover, I drove carefully home and went to bed.

৯৯৯

I would often go up to Rocky Butte to sit and think. It was a peaceful place with beautiful views of Portland, as well as Mount Hood towering in the distance. So on a Wednesday evening, a couple of weeks after the near-suicide attempt on the bridge, I drove up there for some needed peace, quiet and perspective. Usually I would drive up the south side and come home the same way. But this time, when I left, I decided to take the north route down, just to see where it led.

# Resound

As I rounded a bend, I came across one of the largest buildings I had ever seen. The parking lot was packed with cars.

*You need to go in there.*

It was a voice guiding me again, but it wasn't the voice of accusation. It was the gentle voice that had told me I had hope. It was nothing more than a whisper.

I parked my car and followed the urging inside the building. It seemed to be some kind of church, though it wasn't like any church I had ever been to. People greeted me as soon as I walked in, shaking my hand, giving me a hug.

"Welcome!" They smiled broadly, as if they were genuinely pleased I had come.

I felt awkward, so I found a seat in the back. The service began, and I didn't understand much, since the meeting was in English. I was confused, but I was also intrigued by the peace I felt, so I stayed rooted to my seat. After the preacher gave his sermon, two guys came over to talk to me.

"Do you want Jesus Christ in your heart?" The young man knelt down next to the pew where I sat, and he looked me right in the eyes.

I shook my head. "I don't know Jesus Christ."

"Come with me, and I will pray with you," the other man offered, pulling me to my feet.

Even though I didn't fully understand what they were saying, I felt compelled to know this Jesus.

I walked nervously to the front of the auditorium.

# The Drive for Freedom

There were at least 100 people up there, all praying with sincerity and urgency for one another. As soon as I got to the front, five men came over and surrounded me, along with the guys who had brought me up. I felt like I should lift my hands in the air, so I did. The people prayed loudly to God, and I couldn't understand a word of it. But something invisible fell off of me right then. I felt lighter somehow — free from my burdens. And, boy, did it feel good.

ॐॐॐ

I started attending the church by Rocky Butte as often as I could. Even though I didn't always understand the sermon or what was being said, I liked how the people treated me. They were so friendly! They gave firm handshakes and sincere hugs, which to me meant that I was worth something to them. They took me out for coffee, even though I could barely make conversation. They *cared* for me. It had been a *long* time since someone had cared for me.

I began to understand that it was God who had filled these people with such love. God had kept me from killing myself on that bridge. God had cared so much about me that he led me to this church. And God had set me free from my invisible chains.

Over the months that followed, the people in the church taught me about Jesus Christ, God's son, who was sent to earth to take our punishment for all of the evil things we had done. The obvious thing to me was that I hadn't done anything to deserve that. And yet, as the Bible reads in Romans 5:8, "But God demonstrates his own love for us in this: While we were still sinners, Christ died for us."

*While I was still sinning, Christ died for me.* While I was still running away from home and drinking heavily and going to strip bars and doing whatever I wanted … Christ died for me.

He took it all away — our sins, our shame — and all we had to do was accept it. Believe it. And then we would be free. It sounded pretty simple.

One Sunday after church, I went to a restaurant for lunch where I ordered my meal and a beer. Even though I was feeling so much better about my life, I still drank heavily. But as I sat in the booth with my beer in my hand, something clicked. I remembered that I used to call my uncles hypocrites for the way they would go to church and then come home and beat their wives. I didn't want to be like them. I wanted to be different. I knew that my addiction to alcohol was something that had been plaguing me since I was 7 years old. My guilt and self-condemnation about drinking were keeping me from a real relationship with God.

*God, please help me to detest the liquor!* I cried out silently, placing my head in my hands. *I don't want to drink anymore!*

And gently but firmly, I pushed the glass of beer to the other side of the table.

# The Drive for Freedom

❧❧❧

I decided that if I was going to continue to grow as a new Christian, I needed to go to a Spanish-speaking church, where I could learn about my new faith without having to deal with the language barrier. I got involved with a great youth group and, after a few months, made plans to go on a trip with them down to a convention in Los Angeles. I was to be one of the drivers.

But the day we were supposed to leave, someone stuck a screwdriver in my tires. I was so angry and frustrated. I didn't have time or money for this kind of thing! I took the car down to Costco to replace the tires, only to see that Costco was closed — at 4 p.m. on a Saturday. I was beyond irritated. I called the young man in charge of the youth group.

"I'm sorry. I can't go on the trip. Costco is closed, so I can't get my tires fixed."

"Costco can't be closed on a Saturday afternoon! This is their busiest time of the week!" The pastor was incredulous.

"I know. But they're closed." I sighed, my eyes fixed on the auto repair entrance, which was clearly not opening anytime soon.

I thought the conversation was over. I wouldn't be going to California after all.

"Carlos, we need to pray."

The youth leader led me in prayer and then hung up to call Costco, while I continued to pray, my eyes shut tight.

After a minute, he called me back. "Carlos, I don't know what you were seeing, but Costco's open!"

I glanced up, and there in front of me was a busy, bustling auto repair shop.

*That's crazy! This better be some life-changing convention that the devil doesn't want me to experience!*

That was the only reason I could think of why everything in the world would be working against my ability to get down there.

The tires fixed, we set off for Los Angeles, driving down in an eight-vehicle caravan. But while we were there, my radiator broke down, causing me more expense and frustration. The trip was an absolute disaster for me. To make things worse, I sat through the entire convention and got nothing out of it. I was bored and irritated, and I just wanted to go home.

I was grumpy during the trip back to Portland. I had three kids in my car, and they laughed all the way, telling jokes via walkie-talkie with the kids in the other vehicles. Even at 1 a.m., they were so carefree, and there I was — so serious and crabby.

*God, I want to be like these people!* I cried inwardly, as my car sped across the Oregon state line. *I want to be happy like they are!*

Just then, almost in answer to my prayer, a shooting star streaked across the night sky. I knew without a doubt that God had heard me. I dissolved into tears, crying like a baby. I didn't know exactly why I cried, but I definitely felt the power of God in my body like I had never felt it before.

# The Drive for Freedom

"Carlos! There's a dove over your head!" one of the kids exclaimed.

"Yes, I see it, too!" another chimed in.

"A dove? Like a bird?" I sobbed.

"Yes! Like the one that appeared when Jesus was baptized by John the Baptist!"

I remembered that story in the Bible. I had learned that the dove was a symbol of the Holy Spirit, sent from God to be our comforter and helper.

I started crying even harder. The Holy Spirit was working inside me, and I didn't want it to stop. I began to pray, pouring out my heart to the God who created me. I kept driving my car up I-5 in the middle of the night, tears streaming down my face, prayer and praise to God flowing from my mouth. I felt peace, joy and power, all wrapped up together like a wonderful package in the depths of my being.

And then God spoke to me: "Just keep doing what you're doing. I will take control of the car."

The kids in my car gasped and watched incredulously as the car flawlessly rounded the next curve. For the next three hours, God drove my car while I continued to weep and pray. He was doing some intense work on my heart.

When we finally pulled over at a rest stop, I stumbled out of the car and knelt at the nearest light post.

"God, I'm so sorry for all I've done wrong," I said, weeping. "I'm ready for you to take complete control of my life."

But based on the events of the prior three hours, it

sounded like he already had. He was just waiting for me to let go.

༄༄༄

A light came on that night, and from then on, I had a longing to share Jesus with everyone I met. He had changed my life and made me a new person, so I wanted other people to understand what he could do for them.

With God's help and strength, I have not had an alcoholic drink in five years. My depression was gone, and I was filled with peace and joy. Of course, I still had bad days occasionally, but for the first time I understood that Jesus forgives all my sins — past, present and future. Not only had he died for my sins, but he rose from the grave! There was amazing, life-changing power in this real relationship with God. There was freedom from the chains of self-destruction that had held me for so long.

I got a new job as a laser operator for circuit boards, and the job required that I be able to read English. So I took an online language course that really helped me. After I felt better about my English skills, I started reading my Bible in English so that I would be able to share Jesus with my co-workers better.

I became a leader in my church and was eager to help out wherever I could. Over the course of the next year, I became a small group leader, musician, deacon and usher. I really enjoyed being used by God.

# The Drive for Freedom

Our church was looking for another church that would let us use their facility for water baptisms. We finally found one, and we held our baptismal service there. In the process, I fell hard for a bubbly brunette named Katie. We started hanging out, and it didn't take long for me to realize that she was the one I wanted to marry. But unfortunately, we fooled around, and Katie discovered she was pregnant. We moved up the wedding and got married five months before our son was born. But when the church found out, I was taken out of all my leadership positions. It was really difficult, but of course, I understood.

In the meantime, my job found out that my Social Security number was fake. I was still illegal, and unfortunately they had to lay me off. Just like that, I was now unemployed and responsible for supporting a family of three.

"You're a good worker, Carlos," my boss said, regret in his voice. "I will write a letter for you so that you can work somewhere else. As soon as you have your papers, come back, and I will have a job for you."

I started the process of getting my legal documentation, but it looked like it was going to be quite an ordeal. For starters, I was told I had to go back to Mexico for a week. But since Katie was due with our second son, we waited until two weeks after he was born before the four of us entered Mexico through El Paso,

Texas. We stayed with a friend of a friend in Juarez. I worked on getting the documentation I needed, but I quickly found out that it wasn't something that could be done in a week's stay. In fact, they actually required that I stay in the country four months to a year. The other bad news was that we had just run out of money.

That night, we spent a lot of time crying and praying. We had filled out petitions and written letters; we had done everything we knew to do. So we called our pastor in Portland, and the church sent $300, which was enough to get us to Mexico City, nearer to my family.

Over the next few months, I decided to make the most of my time there. It was wonderful to be reunited with my family again and to put the past behind me. My family needed Jesus as much as I had, so I shared with them every chance I got.

"Carlos, do you want to go to the bar with us?" My brother slapped me good-naturedly on the back.

"No, thanks, I don't drink anymore."

"Yes, you do!" he insisted. "You used to drink more than all of us put together, and you were just a kid!"

"I know." I smiled. "But Jesus has changed my life. He has helped me not to drink."

Some were willing to listen, and others weren't. But I knew that it was a start. One of my sisters called me a hypocrite, then apologized to me a month later after God had worked in her heart. She ended up accepting Jesus.

While spending time with my parents, I noticed that my mom's hands shook while she worked — a complication of being a diabetic. "Mom, may I pray for you? For the tremors?"

"Sure." She shrugged.

The next day, I asked her if she felt any different.

"No." The answer was short and curt.

"Are you sure? Didn't you shake a lot in your hands?"

My mother's warm brown eyes grew wide as she studied her work-worn hands, now calm and still.

"Yes, I do feel different!"

Though she didn't accept Jesus right then, I told her that God loves her and that he cares for all the things in her life. I was confident that God was working in my family, and I knew that maybe these months in Mexico were for the greater good after all.

I believed with all my heart that God's grace was for everyone. I liked a particular Bible story about Peter, who was one of Jesus' Jewish followers, and how God helped him to become impartial toward non-Jewish people: "Then Peter began to speak: 'I now realize how true it is that God does not show favoritism but accepts from every nation the one who fears him and does what is right'" (Acts 10:34-35). Jesus died for *everyone* — Jews, Americans and Mexicans, alike.

The scripture went on to say that Peter baptized everyone in Cornelius' household, even though they were of a different race and background. I held onto that scripture as I hung out with my family. How wonderful it would be if someday my *entire household* believed in Jesus. That extended to my father as well, whom I had learned to forgive. I knew that if my dad ever came around, his influence could cause the entire village to follow.

After four and a half months, with some help from an attorney working with the consulate's office, we were given a small window of opportunity during which we could re-enter the United States. Katie and I packed up our two small children and our few belongings, and we made a marathon trip back up to Juarez and were back in Texas (legally this time) within 24 hours. We were homeward bound!

☙☙☙

When I got back to Portland, I called my former boss, and he gave me my old job back for the same pay. He had been so supportive of my efforts to become legal, calling me every month for two years to ask if I had my papers yet. Then, two months after I went back to work for him, he gave me a raise.

Things seemed to improve quickly for us after that. We bought a house and had our third child, a baby girl. Then, in 2007, I finally gained my United States citizenship.

We became more active in our new church, Resound, where we led a small group for new believers. Our love for Jesus broke the barriers that made it hard to get to know other people in our church. Resound became a place for us to share our story and to open our hearts. Though we weren't perfect, God had given us a loving group of friends who encouraged us to love Jesus and to continue to grow in our relationships with him.

I was hungry to learn even more about the Bible, so I enrolled in Bible college. I had so much love in my heart for the Hispanic community and wanted to let them know God loves them.

I believed that in times of need, people easily make wrong decisions, all because they don't really understand God's love. The more I could learn, the more I could teach and boldly explain to others what I had already experienced in my own heart.

༄༄༄

"Dad, you caught one!" my older son exclaimed, setting down his fishing pole and running over to take a look.

"I know! It's a nice one, too!" I held the fish up on the line for the rest of the family to admire. It was a beautiful trout, the first fish I had ever caught in the United States, and much bigger than the little ones I used to catch in the river in Mexico.

Camping and lake fishing was a wonderful way to celebrate the Fourth of July weekend with Katie and the kids. It was so peaceful up here at the lake, surrounded by tall pine trees, miles away from our busy lives in the bustling city. And while the United States celebrated her birthday — our freedom — I thanked God for setting me free from my alcohol addiction … my loneliness … the rebellion in my heart.

I sat down on a log and took a knife to my fish, cleaning and gutting it the way I had been taught as a kid. After 30 years, I still remembered how. My mouth watered with anticipation as I imagined what it would taste like after being cooked over an open fire.

The unpleasant task done, I straightened up and looked back toward the shore where the boys were busy re-baiting their hooks and Katie chatted with our precious daughter. My life with these beautiful people was more amazing than I ever could have imagined, more incredible than I deserved.

When I had set out to cross the border as a headstrong teen, I had hoped for a better life. But I could not have known where that journey was *really* leading me. I had not understood that while I sought physical freedom, God's desire was to go even further — to set me free on the inside and make me a new person. When the chains finally fell off, I found myself freer than I had been the morning I climbed out of the car trunk in Los Angeles.

It was a more complete freedom — better, purer — a kind of freedom designed by God for each and every one of us.

# Scrum
## The Story of Luke Reid
### Written by Arlene Showalter

Air escaped in urgent staccato beats from her lungs as Mum desperately gripped the fingers that wrapped her neck. Gasping through purple lips, she tried prying the hands from their deathly position, trying everything she could with measly half-breaths to free herself from her familiar captor.

But the enraged figure fiercely held his ground, filled with an unexplainable anger that burned for no reason at all. His eyes were wild and vacant, and his knuckles whitened with every breath she took.

*Lord,* her words nearly echoed through the widening whites of her eyes, *please just protect my boys.*

At age 2, I didn't realize my mum was nearly strangled to death by the man I called my father.

৯৯৯

After violence had terminated Mum's first marriage, she had stepped with confidence into a relationship with Dad.

His stellar credentials included associate pastor of a vibrant church, and by all accounts from those who knew him, Dad was a "godly" man — one with the ability to even heal others.

In our hometown in New Zealand, he had one time prayed for God to restore the sight of a man with one glass eye. In a miracle that soon appeared in the local newspaper, the man responded to Dad's prayer with the ability to once again see! Readers were baffled, and the community was stumped. Those in the church viewed his miracles as just that — healings from a man who was obviously following a powerful God.

Husband and father, pastor and friend, the dynamic man successfully lived two lives, public and private — very, very private.

While serving as a pillar of the church, married and fathering three sons, Dad's secret life had included fraternizing in massage parlors and tripping on drugs.

And then, the year I turned 2, attempting to murder my mum.

Dad was one of four men who entered and exited my brothers' and my lives like busy shoppers through a retail revolving door. With men like these, my brothers, my mum and I quickly learned to bind together.

We conducted life like we played our favorite sport. We were a rugby team. Rugby plays require an extreme level of teamwork. For example, during a *scrum*, the eight forwards of one team *bind on*, meaning they wrap an arm around their mates, even grabbing the jersey on the other side to make a tight connection, and press together as one being, pushing against the eight forwards of the opposing team. This takes a great deal of skill, strength, timing and, most importantly, teamwork.

# Scrum

Mum and her four boys were that scrum-forming team. With every crisis we "bound on," bound together and forged forward like the strong single unit we knew we'd have to be.

~~~

"Boys, this is Steve." Mum introduced us to the tall man by her side. It had been two years since Dad had fled the family — time that offered us a chance to grow even closer to the woman who held us all together. All of us would have done anything to see her smile. "Steve, this is Paul, my eldest, and David and Luke." She grinned. "We're getting married!"

Understanding escaped my 4-year-old mind, but Mummy's happiness spilled across her three sons. We loved him for loving her.

But behind the roses and chivalry lurked a brutal beast. Not long after the marriage began, Steve started beating my older brothers, 7-year-old Paul and 5-year-old David, with a broom.

And he beat Mum. She put up with it because flowers, soft music and apologies always followed the tattoo of fists. And, along with the bruises, Steve gave Mum her fourth son.

One day we found Mum poured out on the kitchen floor, beaten and weeping. My child's heart churned with anger and bewilderment. *How can this loving man turn into such a raving monster?*

# Resound

Mum clung to the marriage for the loving side of him and dodged the violent side until the day she came home unexpectedly. Dropping her handbag on the kitchen table, she moved down the hallway, her high-heeled shoes clicking her progress.

She opened the bedroom door.

There lay her husband, Steve, with another woman.

With a shriek, Mum yanked a shoe from her foot, dashed to his side of the bed and scored a heel into his temple.

Mum's third marriage ended after that trip to the hospital.

*He deserved that,* I thought.

༜༜༜

With all the fake and faithless men who had joined and betrayed our family, Mum decided it was important that we meet a man we could trust. In the absence of a stable physical father in our lives, she deliberately surrounded us with strong male role models, taught us about the value of integrity and introduced us to a man she knew would never cheat, lie or kill.

I was sitting on my bunk after dinner, playing with a transformer toy the night Mum came in for a chat.

"How's it going, son?" she asked, sitting next to me and draping an arm about my shoulders.

"Okay," I said, hands busy changing my superhero to a truck and back again.

# Scrum

"You like that toy?" she asked.

"Yes," I responded, eyes glowing. "It's so super cool how it changes."

"Meeting Jesus is like that," she said. "I was a mess before I met him, especially in my heart. See how your toy changes from one thing to something completely different?"

I nodded.

"That's how it was when I met Jesus. I was so angry and confused, tripping on drugs, trying to find my way in life." She paused.

"One day I was walking to a dealer's to get more drugs. A street preacher stopped me and started telling me things about myself nobody else knew. I freaked out."

Her shoulders lifted. "How could this stranger know these things? I told him to go away. But that night, Jesus came to me, in all my mess." She smiled.

"I experienced his total love. He transformed me. I gave my whole heart to him right then and there. That means I made a decision that I wanted to stop living for me and start living for him. I'll never stop loving him."

Mum's eyes lit up, and I could almost see the physical change in her demeanor when she talked about her life after an introduction to Jesus.

"I want to do that, too," I told her.

"You want to give Jesus your heart?"

"Yes, Mummy."

"And have him change you from one thing to another?"

I nodded again. Even at that young age, I sensed my mummy had a special, special relationship with Jesus. She was different from most people I knew, and I wanted what she had.

"Well, Luke, let's just ask Jesus into your heart, right now."

"I'm ready, Mummy."

෪෪෪

Between her duties as single mother and family team captain, Mum ran a successful greenhouse business in Auckland.

When I was about 9, she felt she needed a break and arranged for Jane, a trusted friend, to watch her four sons while she vacationed on one of New Zealand's many islands with another friend.

"Come on, boys," Jane called. "Let's go for a ride. I'm going to teach Mary how to drive."

The two women sat in the front seat with Paul and me in the back. Dave and Matty sat and played in the rear compartment of the station wagon. Nobody wore seat belts.

Passing through an intersection, Mary hit the accelerator rather than the brake. The car hit a pole. Matty and Dave were thrown against the backseat but suffered no injuries. A screaming ambulance rushed Paul and me to the hospital.

Because I was covered in blood, the nurses frantically

snipped away all my clothes. They soon discovered my nose was the source of most of the blood. In addition, I suffered a minor concussion.

Before my discharge, nurses wheeled Paul in and parked his gurney next to mine.

"Hey, Paul, what's going on?" I asked.

He looked at me with a strange, vacant look, totally unresponsive to my question. A short time later, the doctors delivered their somber verdict: Paul had suffered major brain damage.

Someone telephoned Mum, and she returned on the earliest flight. Within minutes, she stormed the waiting room, filled with stunned family and friends, and took command.

"My Jesus has never failed me yet," she declared, "and he's not going to now." She led the entire group into fervent, believing prayer.

In the midst of this storming-heaven's-gates-power-charged prayer, I looked up and saw Paul sauntering down the hall toward us.

My jaw dropped. I looked at Mum. I looked back at Paul.

Nurses and doctors poured into the waiting area, voices bubbling in a hubbub of disbelief, how-is-it-possible amazement … and joy.

*Mum's right,* I knew right then. *Jesus never fails.*

෴෴෴

# Resound

Mum's business grew as fast as her well-tended plants. She needed a sitter for her younger sons and hired an older teenager named Adam.

We got on well with Adam until the day he dropped his pants in front of me.

"Have a look on this," he said.

"Uh, no thanks," I replied, scooting toward the door.

"Come back here!" he yelled.

I ran as fast as a blindside winger with the shed behind our house as my goal. I didn't stop until I reached the safety of the roof. I perched there, waiting for my mum to come home.

Adam's corpulence kept him on the ground.

"Son, why are you up there?" Mum called up to me.

I hollered down my story. She called the cops. They came and removed the perp.

"It's your fault! It's your fault!" Adam screamed as they led him away.

Mum put an arm around me after I shimmied back to earth.

"He's lying, Luke. You did nothing wrong."

*Thank you, God, he didn't lay a finger on me.*

&#8667;&#8667;&#8667;

"I've spent far too much time away from you boys," Mum said. "I'm going to sell my business so I can be with you."

When the money ran out from the sale, we descended

from comfort to want, but that didn't shake Mum's faith, not in the least. Need pulled us even closer as a team.

One day we sat in an empty kitchen, at a table devoid of food.

"Sons, it's time for a family meeting," Mum said, "to pray for food. What shall we pray for?"

"I want burger rings!" exclaimed 7-year-old Matty. This is a sort of chips in New Zealand.

We each expressed what sort of food we wanted.

"And Pickles needs cat food," Paul added.

After our prayer time, Mum went out to check the mailbox. A stranger pulled up in her car.

"I don't know why I'm here," the lady began, "because you don't look like you are in need, but …"

Mum never looked needy. Neither did her sons.

"God impressed upon me to buy food," the woman continued. "And cat food. I don't even have a cat!"

She handed the package to Mum and drove off. Matty's burger rings sat on top.

*Jesus gives specific answers to specific prayers,* I mused as I munched on our God-delivered meal. *Jesus must be real.*

అ✿✿✿

"Did you hear that noise last night?" Matty asked. Due to our reduced income, the new neighborhood wasn't the best, and we were always hearing suspicious noises.

Paul, the eldest at 12, called a team huddle. "We need

to find a way to protect ourselves from possible burglars," he began.

"Yeah, we'd be an easy mark," remarked 10-year-old Dave. "People gotta know Mum's the only parent here."

"Let's rig something up," I suggested.

"With trip wires," Dave added.

"And lots of noise," Matty put in.

We created an elaborate alarm system by running wires to the stereo and more to a box of spoons and various other obstacles.

One night the spoons crashed, and the stereo blared. We all flew out of bed while Mum called the cops. An intruder was caught.

We were too excited to be scared. Our system worked!

What did the intruder tell the cops? "I knew it was a single-parent home with young children. I thought it an easy hit."

Mum's team: 1. Perpetrator: 0.

പ്പെപ്പെ

We loved life. Mum gave us full freedom for boyish creativity. We carved up our backyard into obstacle courses. We rigged up swings high enough to touch heaven.

Paul and I joined the scouts. When I was 10, the organization held a world jamboree in New Zealand. Tents from diverse countries marched with precision across a massive field. Australia's representatives camped next to New Zealand's. Our mum came along to cook and clean during the event.

She met a scoutmaster — a super nice guy named Geoff who owned his own truck and drove for a transportation company … in Australia.

He showed a genuine interest in Mum's sons.

She introduced him to Jesus.

He returned to Australia.

She went to visit.

He proposed.

She accepted.

"Guess what, boys," Mum said upon her return, eyes as bright as her hair. "I'm going to marry Geoff, and we'll all live in Australia."

My heart sank.

*Australia! Is she nuts? What about our friends here? Australia is so big … and hot … and strange! And they'll be teasing us, calling us Kiwis and all.*

Then I remembered … Paul's healing … God's provision … God's protection.

If God provided for us in New Zealand, he must be able to provide for us in Australia, too.

❧❧❧

We boys settled into Australian life like pebbles sinking into a pond. Soon we wondered what we'd ever liked about New Zealand. We made friends, swam, played rugby and loved life.

# Resound

About a year later, Mum worked at renovating the house while Geoff was at work. Paul and I heard a piercing scream moments before Mum dashed from their bedroom.

"Luke! Paul!" Mum screamed. Her hair splashed about her face like red paint as she flew past us to scoop up my younger brother, Matty.

She flung open the back door. "David, get in here — now!"

Mum bounced from one room to another. "I can't believe it, I can't." The sobbing increased. "Hurry, hurry!" she coaxed. "We have to go."

I made a mad dash for our bedrooms, scooping up whatever my arms could carry, while Mum tugged at my shirt, urging us to the door.

"Come on," she cried, snatching up her keys and purse. "We have to get out of here …"

The four of us huddled in the car, each embracing his few treasures, while Mum mashed the accelerator and drove — as crazy as her words.

She drove us to her friend's home, where she blubbered her news.

"Geoff's a … Geoff's a …" she cried, hands to her face. Her bright red hair swung from side to side as she shook her head.

"A what?" Trish asked.

"He's a pedophile," she wailed.

*A what?* My mind raced. Geoff had never touched us — not one of us. We were shocked that this kind

# Scrum

scoutmaster could have done anything to another child.

"How do you know?" Trish asked.

"I was clearing out our bedroom to paint," Mum began. "I found a box and started looking through the files." She wrung her hands. "I can't believe it, I can't believe it."

"You're sure?" Trish asked.

"Yes, the police records were all there," she wailed. "Oh my, oh my."

We dashed back to New Zealand, but none of us was happy. That one year in Australia had spoiled us. We all wanted to go back.

So we did.

Mum enrolled in the social system for assistance. She also took cleaning jobs and later on she became a masseuse, a good one. Money issues melted away.

Through it all, Mum used the experience to teach us where we needed to place our trust — and it wasn't in any one man we could see.

We grew stronger, we built our scrum and our family team got on with life.

My father's mother came to visit us in Australia when I was 12. We had a blast, showing Grandma our new life and world. Grandma loved us all, with total, unconditional love. She loved Matty as much as her three biological grandsons.

Not long after her departure, Grandma sat down to write a letter to us. At that moment, she suffered a heart attack and died.

# Resound

She left each of us, including Matty, equal portions in her inheritance, set aside for our education.

Shortly after that, the phone rang. Mum spoke to my father for the first time since he'd tried to kill her 10 years before.

"You give me the whole inheritance," he growled over the phone, "or I'll hire a hit man."

Mum called a family huddle and gave our team the rundown so we could make our next play. "Your father has threatened my life," she explained. "But I feel it is an empty threat. I'm not scared." She smiled. "I'm not giving him the money. Are you all with me on this?"

"Sure, Mum," we all chorused.

We all knew that if God could protect us from a perpetrator, he could certainly protect us from our father.

ॐॐॐ

We never felt cheated without a permanent father in our lives. Mum had taught us too well that God is the ultimate father. We trusted her … and God on that.

"Always remember, boys," she'd say, "life is an adventure." We embraced her assurance with all our boyish hearts and zeal. We could hardly wait for the next adventure and often found it closer to home than expected.

Mum was deliberate about exposing us to wise and seasoned elders — people who would lead by example in the ways our own fathers could not.

# Scrum

One couple made it their passion to love us and lead us down the right, not just the easy, paths. Fred, a retired pastor, and his wife, Dorothy, took us boys into their hearts and home. And they gently and lovingly mentored us the way our own fathers didn't.

One day, Fred heard Paul telling a dirty joke.

"Come here, boys," he said to the four of us, his voice kind and fatherly.

"Let me explain to you what a real man is." In his own gentle way, he explained integrity, honor, purity and how important it is to love God with all we are and have.

Fred lived what he taught. I respected him and learned.

*This is what it looks like to be a man and lead a family,* I thought. I noted his example and stored it subconsciously in the back of my memory.

❧❧❧

Crouch … touch … pause … *Engage!* Adrenalin surged from my toes to my fingertips as my body strained forward. The moment the scrum half had possession of the ball, I broke out of formation and dashed into play.

Eighty minutes of unadulterated joy flooded my 15-year-old body as I played the sport that had become both my hobby and my family life. The love of rugby pulsated with every heartbeat and oxygenated my every breath.

A few hours later, I flopped, tired but contented, on my bunk and picked up my Bible. Rugby players and

Aussie racing cars sped across my walls in bright posters.

Kaleidoscopic thoughts wove themselves in my head as I read.

*Life is great,* I mused. *I'm young and strong, and today I got to play breakaway, the coolest position in rugby. Matty and I play on the same worship team, there are lotsa pretty girls at school, Mum's work is good …*

A new thought, or sensing, crept into the whirlwind assessment.

*Luke, I want you in ministry.*

My heart stopped … then pounded. Was God speaking to me? And did he want me in ministry? *Young people don't do ministry. It's an unpaid position. How could I support myself?*

The sense stayed … and grew.

My mother wandered into the room.

"Mum," I said, "I think maybe God is calling me into ministry. What do you think?"

Mum's relationship with God was so real. It seemed she held a continuous conversation with the one man who had always been there for her, and I respected her opinion in matters like these.

"Well, Luke, just sit on it, and wait for confirmation." She leaned against the door and crossed her arms. "Allow God to speak to you, and if you're really hearing God, you'll know."

Two days later, a guest speaker came to our church. When he pulled me aside, I knew I wasn't the only one hearing this calling.

# Scrum

"Son," he told me, "I believe God is calling you into ministry."

Two weeks later, another person said the same thing. For 12 months, God sent messenger after messenger to confirm what I felt in my heart: He wanted me in ministry.

ॐॐॐ

Because of her own dysfunctional and abusive background, Mum preferred to leave unpleasant situations rather than face them head on. She moved as often as she changed her shoes. When I was 17, she asked us to do it again.

"I'm done with moving," I protested.

"Think of it as a new adventure," she coaxed.

"Not this time, Mum," I said. "It's my last year of high school, and I want to finish with my chums."

She shrugged. "How will you do it?" she asked.

"I'll get a room," I said. "I need to stay." I wanted the stability of staying in one place long enough to establish myself. So I stayed in Canberra, applied for government assistance and found a room to rent. It took me one and a half hours to get to school each day, but it was so worth it.

The sense that God wanted me in ministry had never left me. But I felt I needed a breather after high school and took a year off. I supported myself waiting tables. Surely, ministry could wait a short summer or two.

I scraped together enough money to buy my first car, which I proceeded to drive like the Aussie racers I admired so much.

My best friends, Ben and Woodie, and I hung out together, talking about girls and fast cars. And we talked to God about our futures.

We camped together, chilled at the beach and had good, clean, albeit not always safe, fun.

"Hey, guys," Woodie said. "How about making a potato gun?"

"Sounds cool," Ben and I echoed.

We scrambled to assemble the proper PVC pipe and couplers, flint igniter, hair spray, cement and a sack of potatoes. After sawing, drilling, filing and cementing, we had a real spud launcher … and a blast.

When the year was up, I moved on to Sydney and enrolled in Bible college.

"Hey," I said to a fellow student, who could pass for my twin. "Name's Luke, what's yours?"

"Luke."

We both grinned and formed a friendship that lasts to this day. I often visited Luke's home, where I met his father, Pastor John McMartin. He took me in as a second son named Luke.

He took his two Lukes fishing, mentored me like a spiritual father and allowed me to see the good, the bad and the ugly of him, freely sharing his whole life with me.

Pastor John taught me what a real man is … and does.

# Scrum

Halfway through my two-year course, I received an unexpected phone call while I was cleaning the youth storage closet at Hillsong Church.

"Luke, this is Mum."

"Hi, Mum."

"I've some bad news for you," she began.

My heart pounded. Vague, formless thoughts careened through my mind. "Who ... what ..."

"Ben, your childhood friend, was killed in an auto accident," she said. "In Melbourne."

I stood stunned, speechless. *Ben? The fellow who could ditch any cop? Negotiate his way out of any situation?* My thoughts raged. *How, how?*

"He was teaching his girlfriend, Angel, how to drive," Mum explained. "She rolled the car."

There, alone in the storage cabinet, I wrestled and prayed.

*This makes no sense to me, God.* My mind recalled all the stupid things we'd done as kids. None of those things had killed us.

As I wept and prayed, anger against Angel rose up. I quashed it. I couldn't blame her for an event God allowed.

I didn't blame God, either. But, at 18, life seemed much shorter. And I knew I couldn't hide from my calling while waiting tables and taking a breather from the real calling in my life.

*From this moment on, Lord, I'm more determined than ever to pour out my life for Jesus. Ben knows I don't have any time to waste.*

# Resound

❧❧❧

I faced graduation from Bible college with some trepidation. *Nobody hires kids for pastorate jobs.*

But God had my back. I was offered a job at Canberra Life Center as a youth pastor. I took it.

*Who am I,* I thought, sitting at a state meeting, surrounded by older, more experienced pastors, *and what am I doing here?* At 19, I was the youngest youth pastor in the country. I felt as though every eye there bore through me.

Thoughts of inadequacy tried to slap me down.

"I'll just stick it out," I decided. "And see what God wants me to do."

❧❧❧

As it turned out, he had a lot in store.

"Hi." The slender beauty with bright bluish-green eyes greeted me. "My name's Alissa."

*She's cute.*

I learned she'd just returned from England after touring Europe. I learned other interesting facts as we hiked together, played sets of tennis or enjoyed chats at local cafes.

*She's got a sweet spirit,* I thought as I got to know her better. *But I want to take it slow. Let's build a good friendship first.*

Nine months passed. *I dig this girl. I love her creativity and her beautiful smile … I'm gonna ask her to marry me!*

# Scrum

I made arrangements for Friend A to pick her up for dinner in Canberra. At least, that's what Alissa thought. Friend A handed Alissa a one-way ticket to Sydney and drove her to the airport.

After the short flight, Friend B picked her up and drove her to a lovely restaurant, located under a bridge.

Alissa arrived, eyes huge with bewilderment, especially at the sight of me in a suit.

I grinned.

"Look at that boat," I said, pointing at the water.

She turned. Friend C motored by, with a gigantic sign hanging from the side of his boat. Huge love hearts encircled the words *Will you marry me?*

Alissa read the sign and turned back … to find me on bended knee, grinning and holding up a ring.

"Yes!" she cried.

We enjoyed a nice dinner, then I drove her to Canberra, discussing wedding plans on the three-hour trip back.

Alissa moved to Sydney after our wedding. I felt my time as a youth pastor was finished and discussed it with Pastor John.

"How about working for me," he asked, "as a young adult pastor? Give it two years, and then I'm sure God will tell you the next step."

"Sounds good to me," I agreed.

Alissa made good money as an interior designer. I enjoyed my work.

Then the familiar sense returned. I had met a pastor

from Cedar Rapids, Iowa, Larry Sohn, and we became good friends. He invited me to check out the United States.

"I'd like to take you to lunch," I told Alissa one day.

"That would be nice," she agreed.

We drove to downtown Sydney.

"This opportunity has arisen," I explained over our meal, "with Larry. He wants us to fly out — no strings attached — for a visit."

Alissa nodded.

"He thinks we're supposed to move to the States."

She nodded again.

A week later, we flew to Iowa. At first it seemed so backward, not at all our style of a city.

But we felt peace — immeasurable, unfathomable, unexplainable peace. We knew that this kind of peace could only come from God.

"This would be a good place to raise a family," Alissa said.

I agreed.

We made the move and immersed ourselves into the American culture. I soon recognized one vast difference between the two cultures: In Australia, folks go to church only if they want to. But here in the States, we've met many, many Americans who go to church, but don't know *why*. And so they miss out on the reality of life with Jesus.

Not long after our move to the States, I experienced the urge to find my biological father, whom I'd not seen or spoken to in years.

# Scrum

"Where's Daddy?" I would ask Mum frequently throughout my younger years. She'd gather me in her arms and hold me tight.

"I'll explain," she'd say, "when you're older."

Mum never hid life from her sons.

"You're old enough now," she had told us one day. "Sit here." She patted the spot on the sofa next to her. "And I'll tell you what happened to your daddy."

I sat down. She wrapped an arm around me, and she told me the story of how Jesus saved her life the day he sent the next-door neighbor boy to her house as my father attempted to kill her when I was only 2 years old.

"Just as I felt darkness covering me, I cried in my spirit, 'God, look after my three boys.' At that very moment, the kid next door walked in the front door.

"'Sir,' he cried, 'what are you doing?' Your father bolted for the door. We never saw him again." She paused, being very specific and deliberate with her next words.

"Boys," she'd said, "that boy had never been in our home before."

The realization of what that meant slowly sunk in, and the God I was just learning to trust as my real father became even more real.

There was no other time the child had ever been to our house. And yet, in the midst of one random moment on one random day that would have ended Mum's life and changed ours forever, a boy mysteriously appeared. Out of nowhere. For no good reason.

"God sent him — and saved my life," Mum said.

# Resound

God loved his children enough to send a child to intercede on their behalf. Just as my earthly father sought to bring about death, the father who never failed sent someone to bring about life.

I leaned back in my chair, remembering the fierceness of her hug that day.

*As always, God,* I thought, *you proved your faithfulness by answering Mum's prayer.*

I leaned forward and Googled Dad's name, hoping to find him and share how full and satisfying my own life was. I found him — everywhere — and read article after article, courtesy of the Internet. *Behind bars for attempted murder.* He was a former pastor, an amazing speaker, a man documented in local newspapers for healing the *blind* — and he had stabbed a man in the *eye.* I shook my head — not in anger, nor shame — but with sadness.

My dad had never defined me, nor had I needed him to fulfill me. Although my mum had failed to find a quality soul mate for her own life, she excelled bringing other souls to Jesus.

I smiled. *She's always been a spiritual pillar to me. Thank you, Lord, for such a mother!*

My thoughts returned to my father, whose bad choices had removed him from ministry. It was no coincidence that I was the offspring of a fallen minister and now myself serving in ministry.

The world would call it ironic; I would call it something only God could do.

# Scrum

The next year, God blessed us with a precious daughter and two years after that, a second daughter. I love being what my father never was ... a real daddy.

&#8766;&#8766;&#8766;

God called us to move again.

"I feel God wants me to plant a church," I confided in my friend Benny. "But ..." I hesitated.

"Hasn't God supplied your need every other time?" he asked. "Why not now?"

His words encouraged me to proceed. After a long period of prayer, God clearly showed us he wanted us to go to Oregon.

Seven of us moved out west and started telling people about Jesus — just like my mum — anytime, anywhere.

We found hungry, searching souls in Starbucks and at the hairdressers. On the streets and at the mall. People began pouring into our home like fans at a rugby match. They filled our couches and lined our countertops.

Churches began offering us the use of their buildings. Less than a year after our move, in January 2011, we launched Resound Church with 360 people.

We didn't come to offer people another church option. We came to love on them.

We came to show them Jesus in action. We roll up our sleeves and get our hands dirty, working anywhere and everywhere there is a need. We show those with hurts, habits and hang-ups that, despite their past, despite their family history, despite their experiences with an earthly mother or an earthly father, the ultimate father came to love them, to save them and to give them abundant life.

# Conclusion

My heart is full. When I became a pastor, my desire was to change the world. My hope was to see people encouraged and the hurting filled with hope. As I read this book, I saw that passion being fulfilled. However, at Resound, rather than being content with our past victories, we are spurred to believe that many more can occur.

Every time we see another changed life, it increases our awareness that God really loves people, and he is actively seeking to change lives. Think about it: How did you get this book? We believe you read this book because God brought it to you seeking to reveal his love to you. Whether you're a man or a woman, an engineer at Intel or a barrista, blue collar or no collar, a parent or a student, we believe God came to save you. He came to save us. He came to save them. He came to save all of us from the hellish pain we've wallowed in and offer real joy and the opportunity to share in real life that will last forever through faith in Jesus Christ.

Do you have honest questions that such radical change is possible? It seems too good to be true, doesn't it? Each of us at Resound warmly invites you to come and check out our church family.

Freely ask questions, examine our statements and see if we're "for real" and, if you choose, journey with us at whatever pace you are comfortable. You will find that we are far from perfect. Our scars and sometimes open wounds are still healing, but we just want you to know God is still completing the process of authentic life change in us. We still make mistakes in our journey, like everyone will. Therefore, we acknowledge our continued need for each other's forgiveness and support. We need the love of God just as much as we did the day before we believed in him.

If you are unable to be with us, yet you intuitively sense you would really like to experience such a life change, here are some basic thoughts to consider. If you choose, at the end of this conclusion, you can pray the suggested prayer. If your prayer genuinely comes from your heart, you will experience the beginning stages of authentic life change, similar to those you have read about.

How does this change occur?

Recognize that what you're doing isn't working. Accept the fact that Jesus desires to forgive you for your bad decisions and selfish motives. Realize that without this forgiveness, you will continue a life separated from God and his amazing love. In the Bible, the book of Romans, chapter 6, verse 23 reads, "The result of sin (seeking our way rather than God's way) is death, but the gift that God freely gives is everlasting life found in Jesus Christ."

Believe in your heart that God passionately loves you and wants to give you a new heart. Ezekiel 11:19 reads, "I will give them singleness of heart and put a new spirit within them. I will take away their stony, stubborn heart and give them a tender, responsive heart" (NLT).

Believe in your heart that "if you confess with your mouth that Jesus is Lord and believe in your heart that God raised him from the dead, you will be saved" (Romans 10:9 NLT).

Believe in your heart that because Jesus paid for your failure and wrong motives, and because you asked him to forgive you, he has filled your new heart with his life in such a way that he transforms you from the inside out. Second Corinthians 5:17 reads, "When someone becomes a Christian, he becomes a brand new person inside. He is not the same anymore. A new life has begun!"

Why not pray now?

*Lord Jesus, if I've learned one thing in my journey, it's that you are God and I am not. My choices have not resulted in the happiness I hoped they would bring. Not only have I experienced pain, I've also caused it. I know I am separated from you, but I want that to change. I am sorry for the choices I've made that have hurt myself, others and denied you. I believe your death paid for my sins, and you are now alive to change me from the inside out. Would you please do that now? I ask you to come and live in me so that I can sense you are here with me. Thank you for hearing and changing me. Now please help me know when you are talking to me, so I can cooperate with your efforts to change me. Amen.*

# Resound

Portland's unfolding story of God's love is resounding here in the Hillsboro and Beaverton area … can you hear your name vibrating with it?

I hope to see you this Sunday!

Luke Reid
Resound Church
Hillsboro, Oregon

# We would love for you to join us at Resound Church!

We meet Sunday mornings at 9 and 11 a.m. at
1400 NE 48th Avenue, Suite 100
Hillsboro, OR 97124

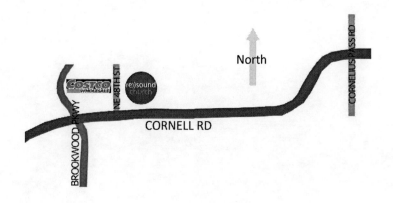

Phone: 503.332.7713

Lead Pastor Luke Reid
E-mail: luke@resoundchurch.com

Youth & Children's Pastor Jordan Smalley
E-mail: jordan@resoundchurch.com

www.resoundchurch.com

For more information on reaching your city with
stories from your church, go to
www.testimonybooks.com.

# GOOD CATCH
# PUBLISHING

Did one of these stories touch you?
Did one of these real people move you to tears?
Tell us (and them) about it on our Facebook page at
www.facebook.com/GoodCatchPublishing.

**S**ecrets sting the air as their confessions pour out.

His wife was gone. Daniel couldn't believe it. Loneliness loomed over his head as sickness threatened to take his life. Would he even survive?

Nina had endured more abuse than she could stand. Her father was a monster, and her husband had walked out the door. She was at the end of her rope. Where would she go from here?

He was an outsider. Carlos had avoided guards and nearly suffocated in a car trunk to find freedom in America. Far from his family, would he ever feel at home?

You'll relate to these seven confessions from real people in Portland.

The mic is hot. The spotlight is on.
The crowd whispers in anticipation.
Listen close.
Hear their voices re))sound.

$14.95

GOOD CATCH Publishing